Aries

1997

by the same author

TERI KING'S COMPLETE GUIDE
TO YOUR STARS

TERI KING'S ASTROLOGICAL HOROSCOPES
FOR 1997:

Taurus 21 April to 21 May
Gemini 22 May to 21 June
Cancer 22 June to 23 July
Leo 24 July to 23 August
Virgo 24 August to 23 September
Libra 24 September to 23 October
Scorpio 24 October to 22 November
Sagittarius 23 November to 21 December
Capricorn 22 December to 20 January
Aquarius 21 January to 19 February
Pisces 20 February to 20 March

Aries

Teri King's complete horoscope
for all those whose birthdays
fall between
21 March and 20 April

ELEMENT

Shaftesbury, Dorset ● Rockport, Massachusetts
Brisbane, Queensland

Text © Teri King 1996

First published in Great Britain in 1996 by
Element Books Limited
Shaftesbury, Dorset SP7 8BP

Published in the USA in 1996 by
Element Books, Inc.
PO Box 830, Rockport, MA 01966

Published in Australia in 1996 by
Element Books Limited
for Jacaranda Wiley Limited
33 Park Road, Milton, Brisbane 4064

Cover design by Max Fairbrother
Design by Roger Lightfoot
Typeset by Palimpsest Book Production Limited,
Polmont, Stirlingshire
Printed and bound in Great Britain by
Cox & Wyman Ltd, Reading, Berks

British Library Cataloguing in Publication
data available

Library of Congress Cataloging in Publication
data available

ISBN 1–85230–820–6

Element Books regrets that it cannot enter into any
correspondence with readers requesting information
about their horoscopes.

Contents

Introduction

Astrology has many uses, not least of these its ability to help us to understand both ourselves and other people. Unfortunately there are many misconceptions and confusions associated with it, such as that old chestnut – how can the zodiac forecast be accurate for all the millions of people born under one particular sign?

The answer to this is that all horoscopes published in newspapers, books and magazines are, of necessity, of a general nature. Unless an astrologer can work from the date, time and place of your birth, the reading given will only be true for the typical member of your sign.

For instance, let's take a person born on 9 August. This person is principally a subject of Leo, simply because the Sun occupied that section of the heavens known as Leo during 24 July to 23 August. However, when delving into astrology at its most serious, there are other influences which need to be taken into consideration. For example, the Moon. This planet enters a fresh sign every 48 hours. On the birth date in question it may have been in, say, Virgo. And if this were the case it would make our particular subject Leo (Sun representing willpower) and Virgo (Moon representing instincts) or if you will a Leo/Virgo. Then again the rising sign or 'ascendant' must also be taken into consideration. This also changes constantly as the earth revolves: approximately every two hours a new section of the heavens comes into view – a new sign passes over the horizon. The rising sign is of the utmost importance, determining the image projected by the subject to the outside world – in effect, the personality.

The time of birth is essential when compiling a birth chart. Let us suppose that in this particular instance Leo was rising at the time of birth. Now, because two of the three main influences are Leo, our sample case would be fairly typical of his/her sign, possessing all the faults and attributes associated with it. However, if on the other hand the Moon and ascendant had been in Virgo then, whilst our subject would certainly display some of the Leo attributes or faults, it is more than likely that for the most part he/she would feel and behave more like a Virgoan.

As if life weren't complicated enough, this procedure must be carried through to take into account all the remaining planets. The position and signs of Mercury, Venus, Mars, Jupiter, Saturn, Uranus, Neptune and Pluto must all be discovered, plus the aspect formed from one planet to another. The calculation and interpretation of these movements by an astrologer will then produce an individual birth chart.

Because the heavens are constantly changing, people with identical charts are a very rare occurrence. Although it is not inconceivable that it could happen, this would mean that the two subjects were born not only on the same date and at the same time, but also in the same place. Should such an incident occur, then the deciding factors as to how these individuals would differ in their approach to life, love, career, financial prospects and so on would be due to environmental and parental influence.

Returning to our hypothetical Leo: our example with the rising Sun in Leo and Moon in Virgo, may find it useful not only to read up on his or her Sun sign (Leo) but also to read the section dealing with Virgo (the Moon). Nevertheless, this does not invalidate Sun sign astrology. This is because of the great power the Sun possesses, and on any chart this planet plays an important role.

Belief in astrology does not necessarily mean believing

in totally determined lives, that we are predestined and have no control over our fate. But what it does clearly show is that our lives run in cycles, for both good and bad and, with the aid of astrology, we can make the most of, or minimize, certain patterns and tendencies. How this is done is entirely up to the individual. For example, if you are in possession of the knowledge that you are about to experience a lucky few days or weeks, then you can make the most of them by pushing ahead with plans. You can also be better prepared for illness, misfortune, romantic upset and every adversity.

Astrology should be used as it was originally intended as a guide, especially to character. In this context it is invaluable and it can help us in all aspects of friendship, work and romance. It makes it easier for us to see ourselves as we really are and, what's more, as others see us. We can recognize both our own weaknesses and strengths and those of others. It can give us both outer confidence, and inner peace.

In the following pages you will find: personality profiles; an in-depth look at the year ahead from all possible angles including numerology; a look at the Uranus Life cycle; *Monthly* and *Daily guides*; this year's Moon Tables; plus, and it is a big plus, information for those poor and confused creatures so often ignored who are born on 'the cusp' – at the beginning or the end of each sign.

Used wisely, astrology can help you through life. It is not intended to encourage complacency, since in the final analysis what you do with your life is up to you. This book will aid you in adopting the correct attitude to the year ahead and thus maximize your chances of success. Positive thinking is encouraged because this helps us to attract positive situations. Allow astrology to walk hand in hand with you and you will be increasing your chances of success and happiness.

A Fresh Look at Your Sun Sign

As a rule, members of the general public appreciate and understand that for practical reasons Sun sign astrology is fairly general, and therefore for a more in-depth study that it is necessary to hire an astrologer who will then proceed to study the date, year, place and time of birth of an individual. Then, by correlating the birth chart with the positions of the different planets, a picture can be slowly drawn for the client.

However, there is also a middle way, which can be illuminating. Each sign comprises 30 'degrees' (or days) and, by reducing these down into three sections, it becomes possible to draw up a picture of each sign which is far more intimate than the usual methods. Therefore, check out your date of birth and draw your own conclusions from the information below.

ARIES (21 MARCH TO 20 APRIL)

BORN BETWEEN 21 MARCH AND 30 MARCH

Your Sun is located in the first section of Aries, which is ruled by fiery, dynamic Mars. Because of this it is likely that you are very typical of your sign. This suggests that you are a pioneer, a guiding light in your circle. In other words a natural leader, mainly because of the fact that you have an overwhelming need to be 'top dog'. Others probably either love you or hate you. It is difficult to feel indifferent to you because you are extremely dominant, enthusiastic, demanding and vital. You radiate life force and because of this some tend to feel a little intimidated. You do have an inclination to barge your way through life, rushing towards your ambitions, be they emotional or career related. On your way you are likely to trample other people underfoot, although you are totally oblivious to this fact and the cost is usually paid by those who love you the most.

This intense desire to be successful no matter what frequently makes for a highly complicated life. Nevertheless, although you may create opposition, it leaves a very small impression on you; and no matter what blows life has in store, you are undeterred and recover in record time, ever ready to do battle once more should it become necessary. Your eyes are set firmly ahead, your path like that of an arrow, and if occasionally you come smack up against the proverbial brick wall, you simply pick yourself up, dust yourself off and start all over again. Certainly you may be a little bruised and bleeding, but you believe that anything worth having is certainly worth fighting for, so you accept that you may become a casualty on occasion.

Romantically, your attitude is very similar. You enthusiastically abandon yourself to playing the game of love. But the game is often far more attractive to you than actual marriage, possibly because you are an incorrigible opportunist and one overflowing with ambition and with enough sex drive to carry you to Pluto and back again.

You are a go-getter and an achiever, not frightened to ask for what you want – far from it. You lunge ahead and seize life by the throat and give it a good shaking. These characteristics are hardly compatible with diplomacy or tact. However, at least you are honest, and, while it is true that you don't always manage to win friends and influence those who count, you somehow manage to struggle through and overcome most things and situations. Basically, truth is your objective. Because of this, whichever way you look at it, you must eventually be considered a success no matter how high the price you have to pay.

BORN BETWEEN 31 MARCH AND 10 APRIL

Your particular Sun is glittering away in the Sun section of Aries. This suggests that you are more emotional, passionate and warm than your brother/sister Aries in the earlier section. Nevertheless, it has to be said that you too are an over-achiever – a person who invariably manages to fulfil your aspirations and even your wildest dreams. Vitality oozes out of every pore and leaves you deliberately searching for competitive situations in which you can shine. Your enthusiasm and inspiration have a way of lighting up your surroundings like a neon sign, no matter where you may be. However, you really can't be doing with the lazier and more sedentary members of the human race. You are inclined to dismiss them without second thought and often with a great deal of derision. At each rung of your ladder you reward yourself with status symbols; these rewards spur you on to even greater achievement.

You are one of the world's greatest organizers, even when or where this talent is not needed. Your capacity for hard work is envied by those around. It is usually the case that those closest to you, despite themselves, are filled with admiration for your persistence and strength in the face of any obstacle. Nothing is going to get you down it seems.

This section of Aries usually brings the fulfilment of most of your goals. How could you fail with such persistent application and hard work. Nevertheless, in all honesty, it has to be said that your demands will fill work colleagues with horror and can also lead to complications in your personal life. You find it almost impossible to think of anyone other than you being first. You are intensely proud, and rash in all situations where your self-image is questioned and nothing fuels your anger more than unfair or unwarranted criticism.

Romantically you are an impulsive idealist, and have probably had more than your fair share of disappointments and knocks. There is a lesson for you to learn here especially where love is concerned. You need a degree of self-sacrifice, which doesn't necessarily compromise you in any way, although you find this difficult to believe. You need to understand that occasionally it is necessary for you to give in to someone else's needs, wants and desires. When romantic problems arise you could be a little bit more giving and understanding: you will be surprised what a difference this can make. At least there is a certain innocent quality to this infuriating, egotistical behaviour. Therefore for the majority of the time others find it relatively easy to forgive and forget.

BORN BETWEEN 11 APRIL AND 20 APRIL

Your own personal Sun falls in the Jupiter section of Aries. You are a much more light-hearted, pleasure-seeking and fun-loving person than your previous counterparts. You are inclined to burn off your excess vitality in some kind of sporting activity. How you love to travel, and you will visit many strange countries. This is because you are interested in other people's customs, idiosyncrasies, ways of life and quirks. Neither are you as all-consumingly ambitious as the usual Aries; you are actually more of a philosopher and a thinker. Because of this there is a possibility that your over-active head will express itself in some intellectual form. A chance to learn and consume knowledge is one of your joys of life. Naturally, because of this, all experience is highly valued.

Of all the three Aries types, you are possibly the most popular and your company is always a welcome addition to any gathering, as your sense of humour is a sheer delight and you have the ability to make life pleasant and fun for all those around. There is no getting away from the fact that you possess contagious charm, which often gets you further than sheer hard slog. Your personality attracts to you friendship, romance and love, as well as a considerable amount of good fortune.

Money tends to burn an enormous hole in your pocket; there are times when you work yourself into something of a lather trying to decide exactly in what direction to throw your money next. However, you have a great deal of money luck, thanks to Jupiter's kindly influence, and this planet frequently comes to your rescue.

Romantically, love games are hard for you to resist, and, let's face it, being loyal or faithful does not come naturally to you, mainly because your compelling personality lures the opposite sex towards you without the necessity for you to make any real effort at all. You could be more helpful and kind, even generous occasionally, as well as more consistent and reliable. However, that twinkling, sparkling personality and individuality mixed with your enthusiasm are usually more than enough to compensate for any selfish thoughts you may possess. Not surprisingly this makes you a sought-after and well-loved person.

WHEN YOU ARE BAD YOU ARE VERY VERY BAD (<u>Horror</u>scopes)

Astrology does its best to explain your talents and your virtues, thus helping you to make the most of yourself. However, it is just as important to recognize the rotten aspects of your sign because, after all, only then can you do something about them. First, let's take an exaggerated view of the evil you, and what you would be like if you were all bad! In plain terms let's take a look at the completely negative side to your character if you can bear it.

In this instance, you will be the kind of character who rushes through life, riding roughshod over kind old ladies and their pet poodles without so much as a backward glance. When driving, it is as if you are taking part in a grand prix. You must be first away from the lights and will spit feathers if cute little kiddies make it necessary for you to stop in order that they may cross the road. Where love is concerned, you are only out for your own needs and victims are sucked dry. Giving love as far as you are concerned is only for fools and maniacs.

Financially you cannot be bothered to concern yourself with such mundane things as overdrafts, or limits on credit cards, so long as you can have what you want and preferably *now*. It goes without saying that you run up debts of alarming proportions and should your innocent white-haired grandmother offer you her life savings, you would take them without so much as a pang of conscience and buy yourself some frivolous item. Where work is concerned you feel you are destined for the top even though you may have no visible talents nor the slightest qualification. Somehow you manage to cover up your ignorance with a lot of boasting, which some mistake as confidence, plus a large dollop of arrogant behaviour. You spend most of your daylight hours and most of the night-time too thinking about yourself and what you want. It never dawns on you for one moment that you are a real pain in the neck.

CUSP CASES

ARIES/PISCES CUSP: 18–23 MARCH

This is a combination of water and fire signs and what happens when you mix these two elements is a considerable amount of steam, which is inclined to make you a weaver of dreams, a fantasizer. At the same time, on occasions, you do spring into action with fervent enthusiasm. An intuitive and a sensitive Pisces hides here with the consuming energy of Aries. However, this does, at least, give you human understanding, and a quadrupled dose of personal magnetism and charisma. This special magic you possess attracts other people to you and they find you difficult to resist, but just bear in mind that you don't always have to let your sensitive emotions take over at every turn. Provided you have been sensible enough not to allow your feelings to confuse your goals, as they will very easily, then you will be able to accomplish most of the goals you set for yourself. Furthermore, Pisces' creativity and inventiveness can make you a fun person in your love and sex life.

ARIES/TAURUS CUSP: 18–23 APRIL

If anyone knows how to get the most out of life it is certainly you. You are luxury loving and always on the alert for fun, trying to cram as much pleasure into your life as possible. Of course the Aries drive combined with the Taurus determination brings you lots of life's goodies, sometimes too many of them. You possess a secret knowledge about how to bring pleasure to your lover. You can be something of an ostentatious materialist, but you choose and display all your treasures with the best possible taste. Your biggest problem, and one which you will fight for most of your life, is anger; unlike most other rams, when your personal volcano blows, the explosion is world shattering. It is invariably felt within a two mile radius and sends those around rushing hither and thither looking for shelter.

The Year Ahead: Overview

You're like a beautiful rocket which flies into the dark of night and breaks into a million stars. This is because you have so much magnetic energy that you attract others to you. You're extroverted, vital and the sort of person others can't resist. You can be a dedicated follower of a cause and are likely to become its spokesperson. You're honest, fiery and passionate and have a great deal to offer other people.

You've so much energy you can probably achieve more on your own than can a group of people. One can never ignore those born under Aries; they make sure you don't. Consider some famous Rams such as Bette Davis, Joan Crawford, Gloria Swanson and Marlon Brando; these Aries couldn't be overlooked – others did so at their peril. Marlon Brando, in *A Streetcar Named Desire,* chose to play a difficult Ram, vital, sexual, but also loud, obnoxious and hell-bent on having his own way. Some Aries, of course, make an equally big impression with their witty brains, such as David Frost and Peter Ustinov.

There's no doubt about it, when your head is on a particular course, no one can stop you getting what you want. You're so determined that even if someone locked you in a cupboard you would find a way of escaping and getting what you want. You like other people who are dynamic, too, and the more successful, the more they meet with your approval. Believe it or not you're far more idealistic and emotional, and even vulnerable, than you look; poor Vincent van Gogh is a classic example of this.

He possessed the Aries energy and determination to do things his way, even though it cost him his life.

The only problem is, Aries, because you're always performing, sometimes you can give those around you a migraine; certainly some of the personalities I've mentioned have been known to cause the odd headache here and there. This is, I suppose, because you have a need for constant praise and will go to any length to get it. Probably the most difficult thing for you to accept is that not everybody wants to hang on your every word. You need to learn not to overwhelm other people with your successes and your ambitions.

So, how is a fiery soul like your good self going to view the prospect of yet another new year? Answer: with a great deal of enthusiasm, daring and determination to achieve as much as possible. It seems, over recent years, that you have at least learnt several lessons. Yours tends to be a Sign associated with selfishness, but you appear to have learnt how to be of service to other people and also how to make the emotional adjustments which are necessary for proper health. Many of you will have discovered ways of learning to relax and may have become interested in alternative medicine. So, what's your lesson to learn during 1997? The answer seems to be that you must rid yourself of self-imposed limitations and slow down a little, because the speed at which you lead your life often proves to be your own undoing. It's a time, too, for serious readjustment of your values and behaviour, and your goal should be growth and greater self-development. Pluto continues to coast along in the fiery sign of Sagittarius creating the chances of world peace and expansion.

On a more personal level, you can expect a great deal of upheaval and transformation; whilst travelling you may change your religion or become interested in foreign philosophies. Other Rams will be determined to improve their minds, and intellectual development is likely through higher education. For you, Pluto suggests activities connected with growth and higher awareness and, in the long-run, this can only lead to a better life. Mind you, it might be a good idea to double-check any kind of travel arrangement because Pluto, when badly aspected, can certainly create some chaos, and this is easily avoided by reading the *Daily* and *Monthly Guides*.

Neptune continues to coast its way through the gritty sign of Capricorn which is, of course, the zenith of your chart. This is the planet of illusion, deception and escapism, which can create a certain amount of confusion where your work or status is concerned, and it's up to you to be as practical as possible in this area of life. When this planet is activated you're likely to experience one of several things, romantic love and light-hearted joy or, conversely, loneliness, apathy and even feelings of futility. Much depends on whether the aspect is good or bad. Neptune's influence is always inspirational so those of you who need this on a professional level will certainly be helped. There may also be times, throughout this year, when you need to sacrifice yourself so that others may get on, which is not an easy thing for Aries being the first sign of the zodiac. It's always important to remember that we're all given choices and whichever way you decide to go when Neptune is in action is entirely up to you.

Throughout this year, the planet of sudden destruction and surprise, Uranus, continues to coast along in the air sign of Aquarius; this planet is connected with originality, genius, eccentricity and independence. Whenever it is activated by another planet you can be quite sure that someone is in for a surprise or even a shock. But at least no one can be bored when this particular planet is around because it makes for startling excitement, which for you is positively electrifying.

Because Uranus is coasting through the friendship, contact and acquaintance side of your life, you could be more freedom-loving, erratic and rebellious in these directions. You may also be drawn to people who are extraordinary in some way; yes, it's definitely going to be the 'different' which is going to appeal when it comes to making contact with others. There's one thing to be said for Uranus which is that once it is in action, life definitely becomes more original and exciting; it's almost like a pepper pot which supplies us with the spice of life.

Now, we have to move on to that heavyweight planet, Saturn, which squats in your sign for the entire year. Saturn is the tutor and the disciplinarian of the zodiac and, because of this, many astrologers consider it to be unlucky. Much, of course, depends on the state of this planet on your own individual chart but, in any event, it always provides us with the chance to learn discipline, accept experiences both good and bad, and in many ways it could be described as a 'teacher'. Certainly it's true that it does tend to bring about some disappointments, delays and, on occasions, depression, but when it is well aspected it provides us with tenacity, strength and discipline, all of which are needed to accomplish anything in life. Yes, Aries, with this planet squatting in your sign, you'll certainly have more determination, endurance and stability during the year ahead and, as long as you finish everything you start, this planet will help to lead you on to great success.

Now for a look at Jupiter, generally considered to be the lucky planet in the zodiac; it's true to say that even when badly aspected he never really brings about impossible situations; certainly, this giant body can make us overenthusiastic, careless and overindulgent, but these are characteristics which you can handle very easily once you've made up your mind. Whenever Jupiter is well aspected you can expect good luck, an opportunity which has not been earned and even greater happiness, so it's certainly worthwhile paying attention to good or bad aspects to this planet in the *Monthly* and *Daily Guides*, for in this way you can take advantage of the jovial influence of this giant of the solar system.

All in all, Aries, as long as you're not expecting an 'easy ride', you will gain a great deal out of the year ahead; this may mean taking on extra responsibility, but that doesn't phase you one little bit, does it? Certainly, the immature Ram will be growing up in record time during this period and will be acquiring a great deal of knowledge along the way.

Career Year

Well, if being top on the totem pole isn't important, you really don't know what is. As a Ram you're not satisfied to be two or three rungs from the top of the ladder of success; you're prepared to work hard and expect to get to the top as your just reward. Apart from the power a good position gives you, you enjoy all the superficial trimmings that go with success; you're not ashamed of this and why should you be? As the first sign of the zodiac, you know you were born to wield some kind of power and to give other people orders.

Worldly recognition is an integral part of your well-being. Regardless of your job, you can't live without it and feel confident or happy about yourself; so you frequently strive towards fulfilling your dreams. In the process, no doubt you drive everybody else around you completely crazy, not that you'd notice, of course, because you're far too busy. You're motivated by a need to be in charge and to order others around; this is because you are competitive, driven and love a challenge. Once you finally sort out in what direction you're going, you carry on regardless of flood, fire or disaster. You sincerely believe that there are so many things to do and such precious little time in which to do them that you don't waste a minute on other things, unless it's absolutely necessary.

It almost goes without saying that you are a leader and an initiator; you certainly give of your best in jobs where you can give the orders rather than take them. You've a head packed full of ideas and a brain that never stops whirling. Your mind is so flexible that you could be anything from a brain surgeon to a beautician, from a writer to an actor. You like attention and, never fear, Aries, whatever you decide to do with your life, you can be quite sure that you won't be overlooked, but will always be respected. You make sure that people know exactly how you feel and think because, if necessary, you'd use a megaphone in order to get a point across.

Now what about the chances of success during 1997? Well, if your job is at all creative, Neptune will be supplying you with sufficient inspiration to make a really big impression on other people. Mind you, there will be times when this planet is badly aspected and, on such occasions, you can expect a certain amount of confusion. Fortunately, aspects move pretty quickly and so, if you use the *Monthly* and *Daily Guides* you will know and understand why you're in such a confused state.

Saturn in your own sign may make some of you groan when, in actual fact, you should probably celebrate. Certainly, you will be expected to work harder than you have for some time, but since when has an Aries like you ever been deterred by the thought of hard graft? Even when impatient, you can understand that the experience is necessary in order to get what you want out of life. What's more, Saturn will be bringing extra responsibility into your life which, of course, can be interpreted as promotion and this will certainly apply to a great many of you. For other Rams though, 1997 may be a year for climbing slowly up the ladder of success in the sure and certain knowledge that all your efforts are going to pay off, if not now then in the not too distant future.

Saturn is the planet which represents experience and responsibility and so, in moments of doubt, which admittedly are very rare, you could do worse than turn to an older person who may be able to put you back on track at the speed of light. Should you harbour a secret desire to change your profession, but feel that maybe it's too late or you are insufficiently educated, 1997 is just the year for taking on extra studies, and for working hard, because eventually you'll be well rewarded.

The position of Jupiter in Aquarius, during this year, will certainly throw a happy glow over all teamwork and won't do the freelancer any harm either, because this kind of Ram relies on contacts and acquaintances and Jupiter will be bringing the right people into your life at the right time.

Pluto, in the sign of Sagittarius, will certainly make for a lively year if you work in foreign affairs, travel or the law. There may be sudden beginnings, transformations and endings, but stay with it, Aries, because eventually such changes will be to your advantage. I suppose the main thing you have to learn during 1997 is to be a little more patient, which is not easy, but don't forget Saturn is there as a disciplinarian and all you have to do is allow yourself to be influenced by its teachings; in that way you can enjoy a successful year.

Money Year

When it comes to this area of life, you certainly relish the game of fattening your bank account, although you are also quite capable, when the mood hits you, of spending as if you were printing the stuff yourself. There are times when you can be a positive danger when out shopping; once you fall in love with an object you simply must have it even though it's far beyond your price range, and this is why you so often suffer from insolvency. Throughout the year there may be times when it is necessary for you to 'tighten your belt' and, when this happens, simply send somebody else out to buy the necessities of life, or don blinkers as you pass any 'glitzy' shops.

When you give in to the impulsive side of your nature, this can cause a great deal of difficulty and pain for yourself and your loved ones, especially when creditors start banging at your door. The worst thing you can do at such times is to pretend it's not happening; luckily, Saturn will help you to face up to the realities of your financial life this year and so you've a good chance of doing relatively well. Whether you're prepared to admit it or not, one of the attractions of money is the fact that it provides you with a certain amount of security; yes, I know this is a boring word but nevertheless it's one that is very close to your heart. You're not so interested in accumulating cash because you want to collect possessions, but you have to admit that you are drawn to money because it gives you the freedom to take off whenever you feel like it. Besides which, money helps you to feel in control of your life, as well as providing a few wonderful moments of sheer indulgence.

But, how are you going to fare during 1997? Well, we've already discussed the fact that Saturn is in your sign; luckily this is likely to make you far more patient where financial rewards are concerned. Instead of expecting to become a millionaire over night you'll be slowing down a bit, taking life a step at a time, sure-footedly heading towards whatever your own particular goal may be.

The planet which rules the area of your life devoted to possessions and cash is the planet, Venus, and so you need to pay particular attention with its placing and the aspects to it by consulting the *Monthly* and *Daily Guides*. For example, during January, Venus will be squatting at the top of your birth chart suggesting that you will gain, but only through hard work; don't expect to win the National Lottery. In February, Venus in Aquarius suggests that friends and acquaintances might be handing on some useful tips, for this is the month in which to swallow your pride and pick other people's brains. Take care in March, because Venus in Pisces suggests you may be your own worst enemy where money matters are concerned and any dishonesty will most certainly be found out. One of the more successful parts of the year in this area of life is during late March and early April, when Venus is in your sign, so the financial reins of your life are definitely within your grip and, whether you succeed or fail, is entirely up to you.

Early in May, Venus can be found squatting in the earthy sign of Taurus, so this is a great time for the collector and also one which will provide you with a chance at least to save a little, so make sure that you do. During June, money is likely to be spent or gained through property in the family and yet another high point of your financial year occurs on 18 August through to 12 September, when, during this time, you will need the influence and assistance of other people, who will be only too willing to put opportunities your way, which will help to swell your bank balance.

For further information read the *Monthly Guide* and take particular note of good and bad aspects to Venus, because this will be providing you with a pointer from the stars as to whether you should push ahead or draw in your horns.

Love and Sex Year

When it comes to love and sex, Aries, you're daring, romantic and sometimes overdramatic. You love to test your 'flirtation' muscles, just to make sure they're in good working order and also, of course, to re-affirm to yourself that you haven't lost your touch. When it comes to love, you want passion, seduction and constant action. You want someone to build up your ego and, to admire your achievements, because without someone to boost your fragile ego, you tend to boast rather a lot. Each romance must be a Romeo and Juliet affair; you're looking for an epic love story such as *Gone With The Wind*. You may not admit it but, deep down, you never grow out of wanting to be blinded by excitement.

Mind you, love isn't always easy for an Aries, because you want to live on a constant high, and so, when things become a little flat, not surprisingly you are strongly tempted by new faces who enter your life. Even when truly in love, you are nevertheless still open to any exciting brief encounter which comes along to grab your attention.

The typical Ram is a strongly sexual creature, and is constantly on the look-out for satisfaction. You want a lover who is completely uninhibited and as straightforward as you. Some Rams have an unfortunate attitude towards love and are attracted to flashy kinds of people who seem to have accomplished a great deal; that's because you don't ever want to be associated with failure.

Certainly where this area of life is concerned you don't waste time; if you see someone you fancy you make a beeline for him or her, make your overtures and, if you are accepted, you're as pleased as Punch, and, if rejected, you shrug your shoulders and move on to your next conquest.

But what about romance during 1997? Well, with Saturn coasting along through your sign it's quite likely that many of you will seriously be considering settling down; this is because some of you feel that you're ready to take on a more serious and stable lifestyle. If you've already found someone special, you could very well be naming the day, or perhaps expecting an addition to the family in the delightful form of a new baby.

For those who are fancy-free, the *Monthly Guides* will prove to be invaluable when it comes to making the most of your year ahead. However, in general, late March through to early April is one of the better times because Venus will be squatting in your sign, which means that you are looking good, attracting like crazy and may simply be falling in love with a resounding crash, like a ton of bricks hitting the pavement.

Perhaps one of the most flirtatious times of the year is during July, when you seem to be so spoiled for choice that you'll probably decide to run multiple relationships. Oh dear! It looks as if you're attracted to a complicated life and this is sure to create problems, though you will no doubt relish the many admirers who seem to be swarming around you.

Mid-August to mid-September is another time of the year when you may meet a very special person; this is because Venus is squatting in your opposite sign, throwing a rosy glow over all relationships. Certainly, if you've decided to become engaged or married, you've picked a very wise time.

For further information read the *Monthly* and *Daily Guides*, paying particular attention to good and bad aspects to Venus and, in that way, you'll be able to make the most of 1997 whilst minimizing any potential aggravation which is generally the idea, isn't it?

Heath and Diet Year

Generally speaking the Ram is as fit as a flea. You have the energy of a marathon runner and your vitality seems to defy human science on occasions and, let's face it, you need every bit because you happen to be one of those people who is constantly on the go. This in itself, though, can be something of a problem because you are loth to go to bed, unless it's for sex of course! For you, sleep is a total waste of time and so you demand much of your cardiac muscles.

You probably realize that your Sign rules the head, and your brain is certainly like a demented carousel which pushes your body past any ordinary person's breaking point. Do be warned that this can lead not only to exhaustion but also, heart attacks. Naturally you are loth to be sick; it makes you bad tempered and difficult to be around. More than likely this is because you are afraid you're missing out on something, and so, the longer you linger in bed the more difficult your behaviour becomes.

Lucky for you, and the rest of us, your health is generally good, although most certainly you have your fair share of headaches. As you know, Aries, when you blow your top, even microbes tend to exit stage right because they simply can't put up with the noise.

Another pitfall of being born under this sign is the fact that you are supercharged and impatient, which means that you want to get from A to B as quickly as possible, and this results in little accidents from time to time. Male or female, you no doubt believe yourself to be one of the best drivers in the world; the only problem is you proceed according to your own basic rules, which are governed by impatience. Those little dents on the bumper are testament to your last impulsive mood whilst travelling from place to place. However, with a little care and caution, you've little to worry about, Aries; you'll probably live to be 150 and still be bossing the rest of us around from your wheelchair as you wield your stick. Mind you, the picture I've just painted is enough to send the shivers down the spines of most Rams.

Now, what about your chances of staying fit and healthy during 1997? Once more we are back with the giant planet, Saturn, which is, of course, squatting in your sign; among the many things it represents are bruises, dental problems, colds and falls, and these are all areas of life in which to be vigilant.

So the first thing to do is ring your dentist, unless of course you saw him last week, although this is most unlikely because, basically, you simply haven't time for sitting around having, as you see it, your molars played with; Even so, Aries, this is a necessary part of life unless, of course, you want to finish up toothless by the time you reach 30, and, vanity would simply not allow this.

Take it a little slower as you go up and down stairs; instead of racing up two or three at a time, consciously slow down and proceed a little more carefully and you'll save yourself a couple of months in plaster. It might also be a good idea to avoid people who are laden down with germs, because Saturn can lower your resistance so that you'll pick up any little microbe which happens to be floating around. There's a chance, too, that Saturn may drain your body of calcium, so make sure your diet is rich in this mineral; step up your intake of dairy products and cauliflower, which is another little-known source of this much needed commodity.

Nobody is expecting you to turn into a hypochondriac, perish the thought; you might just take a little extra care this year; don't, for example, go out into the open air insufficiently clothed, because to do so will be to invite trouble. Surely it's a lot better to take a minute to don a raincoat rather than spend a couple of days languishing in bed with a streaming cold, or even worse, flu.

For further information on health, read the *Monthly* and *Daily Guides* which are particularly good for pinpointing times when you may be accident-prone; a little caution on these dates will save you a great deal of trouble. Whether or not you choose to take this advice is entirely up to you, but, if you don't, why did you bother to buy this book? On impulse? Oh yes, of course!

Uranus Life Cycle

Despite the sign that Uranus was in at the time of your birth, following this happy event, each seven year cycle can initiate changes which correspond with the zodiac sequence. For example, the first seven years represent the time between birth and your seventh birthday, this has a distinctive Aries flavour about it. This is followed by the seventh to the fourteenth year period and that has the distinctive Taurus flavour. This procedure is carried on through the Uranus cycle. Now check out your current age and see whether you are affected by the current cycle that Uranus is in.

0–7 Years of Age: Arian Phase

This is the period of self-discovery and adventure, when accidents in the form of bumps, minor bruises, burns and cuts are common. It's also a time when kidneys and the bladder are highlighted due to toilet-training and this can include problems such as bed-wetting; good judgement by parents is important during this phase. Too much discipline during this period can lead later to health conditions of the urinary tract and bowels, as well as rebellion. Naturally, friendships are formed at this time too, and a child begins to learn that others exist apart from him or herself.

7–14 Years of Age: Taurean Phase

This tends to be a time when popularity at school is prominent as are obsessions and 'crazes'. Fixations on pop stars and other idols, fad foods and strange dietary habits often occur. Destructive, obsessive behaviour such as nail-biting are other examples of intensity felt during this phase. Because of this the throat, neck, tonsils, mouth and reproductive system will be areas of sensitivity and curiosity. This is a phase when it is important that a child learns to share in order to feel secure and loved.

14–21 years of age: Geminean Phase

During this period youngsters are heavily involved in social interaction and learning how to communicate. The hands, arms, shoulders, nerves, sciatic nerve, hips, liver and hormone balance of the body are also emphasized. Mental prowess is tested through writing, reading, examinations, etc. Dance, music, sport can play a positive recreational role and add balance to those who tend to be over-stressed. This is a time when young people tend to be prone to strain and nervous exhaustion or injury to the limbs. It is also a period when adequate sleep and nourishing diet will help to avoid depressed states.

21–28 years of age: Cancerian Phase

This is a period of growing and nurturing. Many become parents or establish their own 'home'. Despite this it can represent an inner battle between parent and child within all of us. In a perfect world it is a time for 'emotional wearning' from parental dominance, which needs to be tackled, but success depends upon the adaptability of parental influence. Those who do not take control of their own destiny during this phase will be the losers and may carry resentment around with them until later life.

The digestion and stomach, metabolism, chest, bone structure, teeth and skin are all highlighted at this time. It is also a stage when we are looking for answers to emotional problems and we tend to over-indulge in food and alcohol. It is a time for being objective in difficult situations – and recognizing the fact that life requires work and effort.

28–35 years of age: Leonine Phase

This is an important period where ambition, personal effort, individuality, vocation and a strong contribution to life in relation to other people are all highlighted. There is also an inclination to overdo everything: the heart, circulation, calves, ankles and back are all vulnerable areas at this time. Luckily recuperative powers are usually good. It tends to be a time when we feel invincible and it must be borne in mind that wise choices must be made and sensible priorities taken into consideration.

35–42 years of age: Virgoan Phase

This is a phase when our food tolerance levels are physically tested. Many people begin to reassess their dietary needs, become more health conscious and take positive steps in reorganizing their lifestyle to match their changing requirements.

This is a time for mental discrimination. Dislikes and likes are carefully examined, but nevertheless, we may still achieve some of our most outstanding work. The spleen, digestive tract, lymphatic system, nervous system and feet may be underlying causes of health problems at this time. Chemical allergies are also a possible source of discomfort and unpleasant symptoms experienced must be examined.

42–49 years of age: Libran Phase

This phase is frequently labelled the menopause or mid-life crisis and can create a mental or emotional throwback to our childhood. This age celebrates the start of the externalization of the wisdom we have gleaned since birth. If we were given free rein and were thoroughly spoilt during our period of freedom and self-discovery (0–7 years) it will be difficult to adapt to others' needs at this time. Many decide to break away and do things their way at this time. All relationships are tested and often fail, sometimes past relationships are even revived. Adaptability should be the key word during this particular phase. The hormone balance, blood pressure, kidneys and cerebral functions are stressed. Conditions such as dizziness, neuralgia, insomnia and headaches can be helped with the right treatment. The flesh will start to lose its elasticity but exercise will keep us in trim.

49–56 years of age: Scorpio Phase

Confusing feelings can accompany this period of life. Whilst the 7–14 phase is concerned with developing the reproductive system this particular part of life is concerned with stabilizing the reproductive system, and generally marks the end of reproduction. The security-consciousness and obsessions emphasized between the ages of 7 and 14 can once again manifest themselves as a fear of ageing, possessiveness and obsession with one's sexual prowess or even lack of it. The bowel, bladder, throat, neck and reproductive system all require preventative measures in the form of diet and attitudes.

56–63 years of age: Sagittarian Phase

This period can be extremely rewarding for the person who is involved in living life to the fullest. Great wisdom should have been attained and will help younger friends and family members. Many of this age decide to travel and consider alternative self-improvement, activities or education. Others regrettably become restless and bored, develop high cholesterol levels and weight problems, nervous anxiety and disorders of the blood and stiffness of the hips and back. During this period it is important to refocus on personal potentials, to live a useful and active life, or we may conclude that we have outlived our usefulness. It's usual at this time for children to have left home and so we are frequently left with a void.

Now is a time to pick up on hobbies that have always fascinated us.

63–70 years of age: Capricornian Phase

This can represent a time of achievement, the peak of a life's work. Many are still productive but others retire and look for an alternative occupation or hobby. It is during this time we reap our health harvest, which is based on how we have treated our bodies in the previous years. The effects of calcification and hardening of joints and arteries may require attention. Common problems are stones in the organs, hardening of the joints, drying of the skin and scalp and loss of teeth and hair. Between the ages of 21 and 28 we must establish our own individuality, between 63 and 70 it is time to let go of others and allow them to develop at their own pace. We must not unwittingly hinder the potential of those we love the most.

70–77 years of age: Aquarian Phase

Oddly enough new motivations and ambitions often arise at this time. Often there is a loss of a partner so it becomes important to become involved in groups, in order to establish new friendships and develop new interests. Unexpected happiness is a distinct possibility if we remain positive to our circumstances and seriously consider the contribution we can make. Many couples in this age group need a refreshing incentive to share new hobbies, courses and activities involving intellectual stimulation. A lack of effort can promote lessened muscle co-ordination and absentmindedness.

77–84 years of age: Piscean Phase

Those in this age group have an inclination to withdraw unless they're wise enough to develop plenty of interests and friends. It is a time of acceptance, sentiment and reflection. Sometimes it is harder for the younger generation to see through the veil of age because it is frequently disguised by ill-health plus a spirit which is still young, and resents the limitations imposed upon us by our physical conditions. This age group should stick to dramatic dietary modification especially in the quantity of food eaten – toxic effects are likely through improper absorption of food. The bladder and general vitality are weakened, and bunions are common. Fresh fruit and vegetables and easily digested nutrients combined with pure water can revive, restore and cleanse the body.

84 years of age and later: Second Arian Phase

Those who reach this great age are likely to experience a desire for fresh beginnings. Some even move or marry at this time. Seven year cycles repeat themselves in what can only be described as a second childhood or at the very least as second wind.

(For further information on the various health cycles in life it is recommended that the reader turn to the *Health Zodiac* by Pamela Row, published by Ashgrove Press, 1993.)

Numerology Year

In order to discover the number of any year you are interested in, your 'individual year number', first take your birth date, day and month, and add this to the year you are interested in, be it in the past or in the future. As an example, say you were born on 9 August and you are interested in 1995:

$$\begin{array}{r} 9 \\ 8 \\ \underline{1995} \\ \underline{2012} \end{array}$$

Then, write down $2 + 0 + 1 + 2$ and you will discover this equals 5. This means that the number of your year is 5.

You can experiment with this method by taking any year from your past and discovering with the help of the following guide whether or not numerology works out for you.

The guide is perennial and applicable to all Sun signs: you can look up years for your friends as well as for yourself. Use it to discover general trends ahead, the way you should be approaching a chosen period and how you can make the most of the future.

INDIVIDUAL YEAR NUMBER 1

GENERAL FEEL

A time for being more self-sufficient and one when you should be ready to grasp the nettle. All opportunities must be snapped up, after careful consideration. Also an excellent time for laying down the foundations for future success in all areas.

DEFINITION

Because this is the number 1 individual year, you will have the chance to start again in many areas of life. The emphasis will be upon the new; there will be fresh faces in your life, more opportunities and perhaps even new experiences. If you were born on either the 1st, 19th or 28th and were born under the sign of Aries or Leo then this will be an extremely important time. It is crucial during this cycle that you be prepared to go it alone, push back horizons and generally open up your mind. Time also for playing the leader or pioneer wherever necessary. If you have a hobby which you wish to turn into a business, or maybe you simply wish to introduce other people to your ideas and plans, then do so whilst experiencing this individual cycle. A great period too for laying down the plans for long-term future gains. Therefore, make sure you do your homework well and you will be reaping the rewards at a later date.

RELATIONSHIPS

This is an ideal period for forming new bonds, perhaps business relationships, new friends and new loves too. You will be attracted to those in high positions and with strong personalities. There may also be an emphasis on bonding with people a good deal younger than yourself. If you are already in a long-standing relationship, then it is time to clear away the dead wood between you which may have been causing misunderstandings and unhappiness.

Whether in love or business, you will find those who are born under the sign of Aries, Leo or Aquarius far more common in your life, also those born on the following dates: 1st, 4th, 9th, 10th, 13th, 18th, 19th, 22nd and 28th. The most important months for this individual year when you are likely to meet up with those who have a strong influence on you are January, May, July and October.

CAREER

It is likely that you have been wanting to break free and to explore fresh horizons in your job or in your career and this is definitely a year for doing so. Because you are in a fighting mood, and because your decision-making qualities as well as your leadership qualities are foremost, it will be an easy matter for you to find assistance as well as to impress other people. Major professional changes are likely and you will also feel more independent within your existing job. Should you want times for making important career moves, then choose Mondays or Tuesdays. These are good days for pushing your luck and presenting your ideas well. Changes connected with your career are going to be more likely during April, May, July and September.

HEALTH

If you have forgotten the name of your doctor or dentist, then this is the year for going for checkups. A time too when people of a certain age are likely to start wearing glasses. The emphasis seems to be on eyes. Start a good health regime. This will help you cope with any adverse events that almost assuredly lie ahead. The important months for your own health as well as for loved ones are March, May and August.

INDIVIDUAL YEAR NUMBER 2

GENERAL FEEL

You will find it far easier to relate to other people.

DEFINITION

What you will need during this cycle is diplomacy, co-operation and the ability to put yourself in someone else's shoes. Whatever you began last year will now begin to show signs of progress. However, don't expect miracles; changes are going to be slow rather than at the speed of light. Changes will be taking place all around you. It is possible too that you will be considering moving from one area to another, maybe even to another country. There is a lively feel about domesticity and in relationships with the opposite sex too. This is going to be a marvellous year for making things come true and asking for favours. However, on no account should you force yourself and your opinions on other people. A spoonful of honey is going to get you a good deal further than a spoonful of vinegar. If you are born under the sign of Cancer or Taurus, or if your birthday falls on the 2nd, 11th, 20th or 29th, then this year is going to be full of major events.

RELATIONSHIPS

You need to associate with other people far more than is usually the case – perhaps out of necessity. The emphasis is on love, friendship and professional partnerships. The opposite sex will be much more prepared to get involved in your life than is normally the case. This is a year your chances of becoming engaged or married are increased and there is likely to be expansion in your family in the form of a lovely addition and also in the families of your friends and those closest to you. The instinctive and caring side to your personality is going to be strong and very obvious. You will quickly discover that you will be extra touchy and sensitive to things that other people say. Further, you will find those born under the sign of Cancer, Taurus and Libra entering your life far more than is usually the case. This also applies to those who are born on the 2nd, 6th, 7th, 11th, 15th, 20th, 24th, 25th or 29th of the month.

Romantic and family events are likely to be emphasized during April, June and September.

CAREER

There is a strong theme of change here, but there is no point in having a panic attack about that because, after all, life is about change. However, in this particular individual year any transformation or upheaval is likely to be of an internal nature, such as at your place of work, rather than external. You may find your company is moving from one area to another, or perhaps there are changes between departments. Quite obviously then the most important thing for you to do in order to make your life easy is to be adaptable. There is a strong possibility too that you may be given added responsibility. Do not flinch, this will bring in extra reward.

If you are thinking of searching for employment this year, then try to arrange all meetings and negotiations on Monday and Friday. These are good days for asking for favours or rises too. The best months are March, April, June, August, and December. All these are important times for change.

HEALTH

This individual cycle emphasizes stomach problems. The important thing for you is to eat sensibly, rather than going on, for example, a crash diet – which could be detrimental. If you are female then you would be wise to have a check-up at least once during the year ahead just to be sure you can continue to enjoy good health. All should be discriminating when dining out. Check cutlery, and take care if food has only been partially cooked. Furthermore, emotional stress could get you down, but only if you allow it. Provided you set aside some periods of relaxation in each day when you can close your eyes and let everything drift away then you will have little to worry about. When it comes to diet, be sure that the emphasis is on nutrition, rather than fighting the flab. Perhaps it would be a good idea to become less weight conscious during this period and let your body find its natural ideal weight on its own. The months of February, April, July and November may show health changes in some way. Common sense is your best guide during this year.

INDIVIDUAL YEAR NUMBER 3

GENERAL FEEL

You are going to be at your most creative and imaginative during this time. There is a theme of expansion and growth and you will want to polish up your self-image in order to make the 'big impression'.

DEFINITION

It is a good year for reaching out, for expansion. Social and artistic developments should be interesting as well as profitable and this will help to promote happiness. There will be a strong urge in you to improve yourself, either your image or your reputation or perhaps your mind. Your popularity soars through the ceiling and this delights you. Involving yourself with something creative brings increased success plus a good deal of satisfaction. However, it is imperative that you keep yourself in a positive mood. This will attract attention and appreciation of all of your talents. Projects which were begun two years ago are likely to be flourishing this year. If you are born under the sign of Pisces or Sagittarius, or your birthday falls on the 3rd, 12th, 21st or 30th, then this year is going to be particularly special and successful.

RELATIONSHIPS

There is a happy-go-lucky feel about all your relationships and you are in a flirtatious, fancy-free mood. Heaven help anyone trying to catch you during the next twelve months: they will need to get their skates on. Relationships are likely to be ethereal and fun rather than heavy going. It is possible too that you will find yourself with those who are younger than you, particularly those born under the signs of Pisces and Sagittarius, and those whose birth dates add up to 3, 6 or 9. Your individual cycle shows important months for relationships are March, May, August and December.

CAREER

As I discussed earlier, this individual number is one that suggests branching out and personal growth, so be ready to take on anything new. Not surprisingly, your career aspects look bright and shiny. You are definitely going to be more ambitious and must keep up that positive façade and attract opportunities. Avoid taking obligations too flippantly; it is important that you adopt a conscientious approach to all your responsibilities. You may take on a fresh course of learning or look for a new job, and the important days for doing so would be on Thursday and Friday: these are definitely your best days. This is particularly true in the months of February, March, May, July and November: expect expansion in your life and take a chance during these times.

HEALTH

Because you are likely to be out and about painting the town all the colours of the rainbow, it is likely that some of your health problems could come through over-indulgence or perhaps tiredness. However, if you have got to have some health problems, I suppose these are the best ones to experience, because they are under your control. There is also a possibility that you may get a little fraught over work, which may result in some emotional scenes. However, you are sensible enough to realize they should not be taken too seriously. If you are prone to skin allergies, then these too could be giving you problems during this particular year. The best advice you can follow is not to go to extremes that will affect your body or your mind. It is all very well to have fun, but after a while too much not only affects your health but also the degree of enjoyment you experience. Take extra care between January and March, and June and October, especially where these are winter months for you.

INDIVIDUAL YEAR NUMBER 4

GENERAL FEEL

It is back to basics this year. Do not build on shaky foundations. Get yourself organized and be prepared to work a little harder than you usually do and you will come through without any great difficulty.

DEFINITION

It is imperative this year that you have a grand plan. Do not simply rush off without considering the consequences and avoid dabbling of all descriptions. It is likely too that you will be gathering more responsibility and on occasions this could lead you to feeling unappreciated, claustrophobic and perhaps over-burdened in some ways. Although it is true to say that this cycle in your individual life tends to bring about a certain amount of limitation, whether this be on the personal side to life, the psychological or the financial, you now have the chance to get yourself together and to build on more solid foundations. Security is definitely your key word at this time. When it comes to any project, or job or plan, it is important that you ask the right questions. In other words, do your homework before you go off half-cock. That would be a disaster. If you are an Aquarius, a Leo or a Gemini or you are born on the 4th, 13th, 22nd, or the 31st of any month, this individual year will be extremely important and long remembered.

RELATIONSHIPS

You will find that it is the eccentric, the unusual, the unconventional and the downright odd that will be drawn into your life during this particular cycle. It is also strongly possible that people you have not met for some time may be re-entering your circle and an older person or somebody outside your own social or perhaps religious background will be drawn to you too. When it comes to the romantic side of things, again you are drawn to that which is different from usual. You may even form a relationship with someone who comes from a totally different background, perhaps from a distance. Something unusual about them stimulates and excites you. Gemini, Leo and Aquarius are your likely favourites, as well as anyone whose birth number adds up to 1, 4, 5, or 7. Certainly the most exciting months for romance are going to be February, April, July and November. Make sure then that you put yourself about during this particular time, and be ready for literally anything.

CAREER

Once more we have the theme of the unusual and different in this area of life. You may be plodding along in the same old rut when suddenly lightning strikes and you find yourself besieged by offers from other people and in a panic, not quite sure what to do. There may be a period when nothing particular seems to be going on, when to your astonishment you are given some promotion or some exciting challenge to take on board. Literally anything can happen in this particular cycle of your life. The individual year 4 also inclines towards added responsibilities and it is important that you do not offload them on to other people or cringe in fear. They will eventually pay off and in the meantime you will be gaining in experience and paving the way for greater success in the future. When you want to arrange any kind of meeting, negotiation or perhaps ask for any kind of favour at work, then try to do so on a Monday or a Wednesday for the luckiest results. January, February, April, October and November are certainly the months when you must play the opportunist and be ready to say yes to anything that comes your way.

HEALTH

The biggest problems that you will have to face this year are caused by stress, so it is important that you attend to your diet and are as philosophical as possible as well as ready to adapt to changing conditions. You are likely to find that people you thought you knew well are acting out of character and this throws you off balance. Take care too when visiting the doctor. Remember that you are dealing with a human being and that doctors, like the rest of us, can make mistakes. Unless you are 100 per cent satisfied then go for a second opinion over anything important. Try to be sceptical about yourself too because you are going to be a good deal more moody than usual. The times that need special attention are February, May, September and November. If any of these months fall in the winter part of your year, then wrap up well and dose up on vitamin C.

INDIVIDUAL YEAR NUMBER 5

GENERAL FEEL

There will be many more opportunities for you to get out and about and travel is certainly going to be playing a large part in your year. Change too must be expected and even embraced – after all, it is part of life. You will have more free time and choices, so all in all things look promising.

DEFINITION

It is possible that you tried previously to get something off the launching pad but for one reason or another, it simply didn't happen. Luckily, you now get a chance to renew those old plans and put them into action. You are certainly going to feel that things are changing for the better in all areas. You are going to be more actively involved with the public and will enjoy a certain amount of attention and publicity. You may have failed in the past but this year mistakes will be easier to accept and learn from, and you are going to find yourself both physically and mentally more in tune with your environment and with those you care about than ever before. If you are a Gemini or a Virgo or are born on the 5th, 14th or 23rd then this is going to be a period of major importance for you and you must be ready to take advantage of this.

RELATIONSHIPS

Lucky you! Your sexual magnetism goes through the ceiling and you will be involved in many relationships during the year ahead. You have that extra charisma about you which will be drawing others to you and you can look forward to being choosy. There will be an inclination to be drawn to those who are considerably younger than yourself. It is likely too that you will find that those born under the signs of Taurus, Gemini, Virgo and Libra as well as those whose birth date adds up to 2, 5 or 6 will play an important part in your year. The months for attracting others in a big way are January, March, June, October and December.

CAREER

This is considered by all numerologists as being one of the best numbers for self-improvement in all areas, and particularly on the professional front. It will be relatively easy for you to sell your ideas and yourself as well as to push your skills and expertise under the noses of other people. They will certainly sit up and notice. Clearly, then, a time for you to view the world as though it were your oyster and to get out there and grab your slice of the action. You have increased confidence and should be able to get exactly what you want. Friday and Wednesday are perhaps the best days if looking for a job or going to negotiations or interviews, or in fact for generally pushing yourself into the limelight. Watch out for March, May, September, October or December. Something of great importance could pop up at this time. There will certainly be a chance for advancement; whether you take it up or not is of course entirely up to you.

HEALTH

Getting a good night's rest could be your problem during the year ahead, since that mind of yours is positively buzzing and won't let you rest. Try turning your brain off at bedtime, otherwise you will finish up irritable and exhausted. Try to take things a step at a time without rushing around. Meditation may help you to relax and do more for your physical well-being than anything else. Because this is an extremely active year, you will need to do some careful planning so that you can cope with ease rather than rushing around like a demented mayfly. Furthermore, try to avoid going over the top with alcohol, food, sex, gambling or anything which could be described as 'get rich quick'. During January, April, August, and October, watch yourself a bit, you could do with some

coddling, particularly if these happen to be winter months
for you.

INDIVIDUAL YEAR NUMBER 6

GENERAL FEEL

There is likely to be increased responsibility and activity
within your domestic life. There will be many occasions
when you will be helping loved ones and your sense of
duty is going to be strong.

DEFINITION

Activities for the most part are likely to be centred around
property, family, loved ones, romance and your home.
Your artistic appreciation will be good and you will be
drawn to anything that is colourful and beautiful, and
possessions that have a strong appeal to your eye or
even your ear. Where domesticity is concerned, there is a
strong suggestion that you may move out of one home into
another. This is an excellent time too for self-education, for
branching out, for graduating, for taking on some extra
courses – whether simply to improve your appearance or
to improve your mind. When it comes to your social life
you are inundated with chances to attend social functions,
such as openings of art galleries and facilities. You are
going to be the real social butterfly flitting from scene
to scene and enjoying yourself thoroughly. Try to accept
nine out of ten invitations that come your way because
they bring with them chances of advancement. If you are
born on the 6th, 15th or 24th or should your birth sign be
Taurus, Libra or Cancer then this is going to be a year that
will be long remembered as a very positive one.

RELATIONSHIPS

When it comes to love, sex and romance the individual
year 6 is perhaps the most successful. It is a time for being

swept off your feet, for becoming engaged or for getting married. On the more negative side, perhaps there is a separation and divorce. However the latter can be avoided, provided you are prepared to sit down and communicate properly. There is an emphasis too on pregnancy and birth, or changes in existing relationships. Circumstances will be sweeping you along. If you are born under the sign of Taurus, Cancer or Libra, then it is even more likely that this will be a major year for you, as well as for those born on dates adding up to 6, 3 or 2. The most memorable months of your year are going to be February, May, September and November. Grab all opportunities to enjoy yourself and improve your relationships during these periods.

CAREER

A good year for this side to life too, with the chances of promotion and recognition for past efforts all coming your way. You will be able to improve your position in life even though lately it is likely you have been frustrated. On the cash front big rewards will come flooding in mainly because you are prepared to fulfil your obligations and commitments without complaint or protest. Other people will appreciate all the efforts you have put in, so plod along and you will find your efforts will not be in vain. Perversely, if you are looking for a job or setting up an interview, negotiation or a meeting, or simply want to advertise your talents in some way, then your best days for doing so are Monday, Thursday and Friday. Long-term opportunities are very strong during the months of February, April, August, September and November. These are the key periods for pushing yourself up the ladder of success.

HEALTH

If you are to experience any problems of a physical nature during this year, then they could be tied up with the throat, nose or the tonsils plus the upper parts of the body. Basically what you need to stay healthy during this year is plenty of sunlight, moderate exercise, fresh air and changes of scene. Escape to the coast too if this is at all possible. The months for being particularly watchful are March, July, September and December. Think twice before doing anything during this time and there is no reason why you shouldn't stay hale and hearty for the whole year.

INDIVIDUAL YEAR NUMBER 7

GENERAL FEEL

A year for inner growth and for finding out what really makes you tick and what you need to make you happy. Self-awareness and discovery are all emphasized during the individual year 7.

DEFINITION

You will be provided with the opportunity to place as much emphasis as possible on your personal life and your own well-being. There will be many occasions when you will find yourself analysing your past motives and actions, and developing a need to give more attention to your own personal needs, goals and desires. There will also be many occasions when you will feel the need to escape any kind of confusion, muddle or noise, and time spent alone will not be wasted. It will give you time for meditation and also for examining exactly where you have come to so far and where you want to go in the future. It is important you make up your mind what you want out of this particular year because once you have done this you will attain those ambitions. Failure to do so could mean you end up chasing your own tail and that is a pure waste of time and energy. You will also discover that secrets about yourself and other people could be surfacing during this year. If you are born under the sign of Pisces or Cancer, or on the 7th, 16th or 25th of the month, then this year will be especially wonderful.

RELATIONSHIPS

It has to be said from the word go that this is not the best year for romantic interest. A strong need for contemplation will mean spending time on your own. Any romance that does develop this year may not live up to your great expectations, but, providing you are prepared to take things as they come without jumping to conclusions, then you will enjoy yourself without getting hurt. Decide exactly what it is you have in mind and then go for it. Romantic interests this year are likely to be with people who are born on dates that add up to 2, 4 or 7 or with people born under the sign of Cancer or Pisces. Watch for romantic opportunities during January, April, August and October.

CAREER

When we pass through this particular individual cycle, two things in life tend to occur: retirement from the limelight, or a general slowing down, perhaps by taking leave of absence or maybe retraining in some way. It is likely too that you will become more aware of your own occupational expertise and skills – you will begin to understand your true purpose in life and will feel much more enlightened. Long-sought-after goals begin to come to life if you have been drifting of late. The best attitude to have throughout the year is an exploratory one when it comes to your work. If you want to set up negotiations, interviews or meetings, arrange them for Monday or Friday. In fact any favours you seek should be tackled on these days. January, March, July, August, October and December are particularly good for self-advancement.

HEALTH

Since, in comparison to previous years, this is a rather quiet time, health problems are likely to be minor. Some will possibly come through irritation or worry and the best thing to do is to attempt to remain meditative and calm. This state of mind will bring positive results. Failure to do so may create unnecessary problems by allowing your imagination to run completely out of control. You need time this year to restore, recuperate and contemplate. Any health changes that do occur are likely to happen in February, June, August and November.

INDIVIDUAL YEAR NUMBER 8

GENERAL FEEL

This is going to be a time for success, for making important moves and changes, a time when you may gain power and certainly one when your talents are going to be recognized.

DEFINITION

This individual year gives you the chance to 'think big', a time when you can occupy the limelight and wield power. If you were born on the 8th, 17th or 26th of the month or come under the sign of Capricorn, pay attention to this year and make sure you make the most of it. You should develop greater maturity and will discover a true feeling of faith and destiny, both in yourself and in events that occur. This is a cycle connected with career, ambition and money, but debts from the past will have to be repaid. For example, an old responsibility or debt that you may have avoided in past years may reappear to haunt you. However, whatever you do with this twelve months, aim high – think big, think success and above all be positive.

RELATIONSHIPS

This particular individual year is one which is strongly connected with birth, divorce and marriage – most of the landmarks we experience in life in fact. Lovewise, those who are more experienced or older than you, or someone of power, authority, influence or wealth will be very attractive. This year will be putting you back in touch with those from your past – old friends, comrades, associates, and even romances from long ago crop up once more. You should not experience any great problems romantically this year, especially if you are dealing with Capricorns or Librans, or with those whose date of birth adds up to 8, 6 or 3. The best months for romance to develop are likely to be March, July, September and December.

CAREER

The number 8 year is generally believed to be the best one when it comes to bringing in cash. It is also good for asking for a rise or achieving promotion or authority over other people. This is your year for bathing in the limelight of success, the result perhaps of your past efforts. Now you will be rewarded. Financial success is all but guaranteed, provided you keep faith with your ambitions and yourself. It is important that you set major aspirations for yourself and work slowly towards them. You will be surprised how easily they are fulfilled. Conversely, if you are looking for work, then do set up interviews, negotiations and meetings, preferably on Saturday, Thursday or Friday, which are your luckiest days. Also watch out for chances to do yourself a bit of good during February, June, July, September and November.

HEALTH

You can avoid most health problems, particularly headaches, constipation or liver problems, by avoiding moods of depression, and feelings of loneliness. It is important when these descend that you keep yourself busy enough not to dwell on them. When it comes to receiving attention from the medical profession you would be well advised to get a second opinion. Eat wisely, try to keep a positive and enthusiastic outlook on life and all will be well.

Periods which need special care are January, May, July and October. Therefore, if these months fall during the winter part of your year, wrap up well and dose yourself with vitamins.

INDIVIDUAL YEAR NUMBER 9

GENERAL FEEL

A time for tying up loose ends. Wishes are likely to be fulfilled and matters brought to swift conclusions. Inspirations run amok. Much travel is likely.

DEFINITION

The number 9 individual year is perhaps the most success-ful of all. It tends to represent the completion of matters and affairs, whether in work, business, or personal affairs. Your ability to let go of habits, people and negative circumstances or situations, that may have been holding you back, is strong. The sympathetic and humane side to your character also surfaces and you learn to give more freely of yourself without expecting anything in return. Any good deeds that you do will certainly be well rewarded, in terms of satisfaction and perhaps financially too. If you are born under the sign of Aries or Scorpio, or on the 9th, 18th or 27th of the month, this is certainly going to be an all important year.

RELATIONSHIPS

The individual year 9 is a cycle which gives appeal as well as influence. Because of this, you will be getting emotion-ally tied up with members of the opposite sex who may be outside your usual cultural or ethnic group. The reason for this is that this particular number relates to humanity and of course this tends to quash ignorance, pride and bigotry. You also discover that Aries, Leo and Scorpio people are going to be much more evident in your domestic affairs, as well as those whose birth dates add up to 9, 3 or 1. The important months for relationships are February, June, August and November. These will be extremely hectic and eventful from a romantic viewpoint and there are times when you could be swept off your feet.

CAREER

This is a year which will help to make many of your dreams and ambitions come true. Furthermore it is an excellent time for success if you are involved in marketing your skills, your talents and your expertise on a broader level. You may be thinking of expanding abroad for example and if so this is certainly a good idea. You will find that harmony and co-operation with your co-workers or those who work for you are easier than before and this will help your dreams and ambitions. The best days for you if you want to line up meetings or negotiations are going to be Tuesday and Thursday and this also applies if you are looking for employment or want a special day for doing something of an ambitious nature. Employment or business changes could also feature during January, May, June, August and October.

HEALTH

The only physical problem you may have during this particular year is accidents, so be careful. Try too to avoid unnecessary tension and arguments with other people. Take extra care when you are on the roads: no drinking and driving for example. You will only have problems if you play your own worst enemy. Be extra watchful when in the kitchen or bathroom: sharp instruments that you find in these areas can lead to cuts being commonplace, unless you take care.

Monthly Guide

JANUARY

This year you seem to have been prepared to get back to work after the New Year celebrations far quicker than is usually the case; this is probably because there is so much activity in the gritty sign of Capricorn, which is, of course, the zenith of your chart. There are no less than four planets in this Sign, up until the 20th anyway, and so the 'workaholic' raises its ugly head, much to the chagrin of your loved ones who are sure to be complaining about neglect at some point if you go to extremes, which you most certainly will because the middle road is simply not the Aries way.

It's a particularly lucky time for those in positions of power or influence; you'll find that other people are more willing to follow your lead and allow you to act as their inspiration far more than is usually the case. So, if you're a boss or a supervisor, this is certainly going to be a fulfilling period. Venus' placing in Capricorn, from the 10th onwards, will certainly be going a long way to helping those of you in professional partnerships or creative work. Mind you, you may have to keep your ego under wraps, just a touch, because if you come over as being too arrogant, you may scare potential customers or clients away. Charm is your best weapon during this period, Aries, so make sure you use it, because you've oodles of the stuff when you decide the time is right.

Take a little care during the first twelve days of the month because Mercury will be in retrograde movement which means that from our position in space it seems to be going backwards. Regardless of your profession or job, make sure that you read contracts and paperwork through thoroughly and, where possible, avoid applying your signature until this planet has had time to see common sense, which is on the 13th. Those of you who may need to travel for any reason at all can also expect a certain amount of complications, thanks to this placing of Mercury, so don't leave anything to chance; check out estimated times of arrivals, departures and connections because, with a little caution, you need not be affected by this mischievous planet.

The first twelve days should also not be used for pushing ahead with legal matters because all this will do is create complication upon complication. You'll notice a drastic change in many areas of life once Mercury resumes direct movement again. Late in the month the Sun will be joining Jupiter and Uranus in the airy sign of Aquarius, placing the emphasis on contacts and acquaintances and so, if you are self-employed or a freelance worker, this is a time for leaping into action. It's a happy time, too, for those who work as part of a team because co-operation will be relatively easy for you to get.

Socially, during the early part of the month anyway, you may be anxious to mix business with pleasure, especially if your work relies on contacts. This could be a good move, because people tend to be more relaxed over a drink or a meal and may give some information which you will later discover to be invaluable. So, the month starts off slowly because of the emphasis on work, but after the 19th you'll be rushing around hither and thither visiting friends, acquaintances and clubs and taking part in team activities too.

Cashwise, because you have the energy of three steam

engines and are working like crazy, you'll be storing financial reward for the future. Yes, it looks as if money may be slow to come in but a slow trickle will soon turn into a tidal wave swelling your bank account accordingly.

Emotionally, for the first ten days of January, you may be drawn to those who come from different backgrounds from yourself or meet attractive propositions while you are travelling. After this date, it's work which may provide you with chances to meet the opposite sex. So, if a colleague invites you out, even though they may not exactly be your best friend, for heaven's sake accept. Mind you, if you're already in a relationship, you'll need to fight the temptation to give in to those sideline attractions because otherwise there could be some unpleasant flack flying around later in the month. During the last week of January, it's friends who'll be making interesting introductions. If you happen to be fancy-free, a visit to a club could lead to a brief encounter, too, but mind you, in the main, you're not out there looking for the love of your life, only for a substitute with whom you can play for the time being. Nevertheless, January certainly seems to be an interesting start to the year and will be providing you with plenty of food for thought for the future. Now for a look at the state of the Moon.

The New Moon occurs on the 9th, in the gritty sign of Capricorn, which is the zenith of your chart. This suggests a minor new cycle where ambitions and work are concerned, perhaps new colleagues for you to acquaint yourself with, or maybe a new ambition which you can share with other people. As you no doubt realize, New Moons can be used successfully for launching anything fresh on to an unsuspecting world. It's likely, too, that plenty of news will be making the rounds within your professional life, though some of what you hear should be taken with a mountain of salt and you will need time to sit down and work out truth from fantasy. Because this particular New Moon occurs at the highest point on your chart, you can certainly afford to push your professional ambitions as hard as possible.

The Full Moon occurs on the 23rd in the fiery sign of Leo; always tricky things Full Moons and this particular one seems to suggest that either a social or a romantic occasion may not live up to expectations or may be cancelled altogether. It's not a lucky time for sport, so gambling should be strictly out, unless you don't mind being broke for a couple of weeks or so. Naturally, though, Full Moons are significant and always particularly lucky for making plans for the future, though not for leaping into action immediately. This is just as well because, as an Aries, you tend to be too impulsive; certainly you lay down the grand scheme of what you want out of life but tend to overlook the fiddling little details, so the Full Moon will provide you with the chance to rethink making sure this doesn't occur.

FEBRUARY

Up until the 19th the fiery Sun with be squatting in the air sign of Aquarius. This is extremely helpful for those of you who work as a member of a team because there's maximum co-operation. It's good, too, for those involved in administration, club activities or work which relies heavily on contacts, so, if you are a freelance worker or are self-employed, you are provided with an excellent time for hustling around and seeing what's available and what isn't. You won't find it difficult to get information out of other people, they're only too willing to be as helpful as they can, which makes a pleasant change, doesn't it?

From the 19th onwards, the Sun will have moved into the watery sign of Pisces, a rather secretive part of your chart, so perhaps you may not have all the pertinent facts at your fingertips and it could become necessary for you to dig around in the background in order to find out what's really going on. Certainly, this is a great time for those in jobs which require investigation or research. And, ideally, during this latter part of the month, you should involve yourself with making plans, or even reviewing old projects that you've tossed to one side, because you may be able to rescue something that once was not viable and now looks as if it suddenly has become quite valuable. Also, during this part of the month, don't insist on keeping a high profile because, if you do, your popularity could sink through the floorboards. We all need one part of the year when we can afford to reflect on things and, although this goes against the Aries grain, nevertheless the latter part of this month is one of those times.

Cashwise, the planet to take notice of is Venus, check the aspects to it in the *Daily Guide*. During February it will be squatting in the sign of Aquarius, between the 3rd and the 26th, which suggests that you can gain once more from your contacts and friends and you shouldn't be too proud to act on their advice. To your surprise somebody could very well repay a loan that you'd more or less given up on. This puts a little extra 'jingle' in your pocket, but not for long knowing you, because as soon as you see something that takes your fancy, cash burns a hole in your pocket. Money will also be spent on socializing with friends but don't fall into the Aries trap of trying to keep up with people who are better off than you are; this is the way down the road to bankruptcy, which I think you may have travelled down before, let's not have it occur again.

Emotionally, you're more interested in finding the love of your life; maybe you already have. The single Ram is about to make as many conquests as possible in as little time as possible; you shouldn't have any difficulty finding admirers, but do make sure that you don't lead them on, allowing them to believe they mean far more to you than they really do. In other words, Aries, it might be a good idea to put your emotional cards on the table because it'll save you a great deal of bother and potential enemies in the future.

The position of your ruling planet, Mars, in the opposite sign of Libra, suggests a certain amount of being accident-prone and experiencing stress. You may find yourself getting into arguments with those who are closest to you; determined to come out on top as you usually are, this is sure to take a great deal out of you. Take care, too, with hot and sharp objects as they are another health hazard. As a fire sign, you like to keep on the go from morning till night and this is especially true right now, but even you need to rest up sometimes, Aries, otherwise you'll find yourself on the sick-list, which may mean you'll miss out on something special, and that would never do. Now for a look at the state of the Moon.

The New Moon this month occurs on the 7th in the airy sign of Aquarius suggesting a strong possibility of your entering a new circle of friends. There's a chance, too, that you may come across romance whilst you are out clubbing and somebody new could be instigating a fresh ambition or objective. As always, New Moons must be used to good effect, bringing disagreements out into the open, adopting a new image or attitude, in fact anything your little heart desires.

The Full Moon this month occurs on the 22nd in the earthy sign of Virgo. Luckily, this happens over a weekend, I say luckily because you seem to be temporarily out of energy for one reason or another. Some of you may even be feeling insecure, very out of character, but not entirely impossible. If so, it is best, perhaps, to rest up and avoid the social whirl for the time being; after all it'll still be there when you decide to emerge at a later date. As always, Full Moons are particularly useful for making plans but not for taking action.

MARCH

Well, Aries, the month starts off quietly enough because the Sun and Venus are squatting in the watery sign of Pisces up until the 22nd; so this continues to be an excellent time for work which requires secrecy, for boning up on your speciality, for making plans and definitely for keeping a low profile for a while. Providing you take this advice, you'll be able to emerge on the 21st into centre stage ready to conquer the world in your usual flamboyant fashion, because after this date we begin your zodiac year, a month when you can make life see things from your point of view. It'll be a great time for those who are self-employed, the freelance worker or even those in positions of authority. Your confidence goes through the ceiling and you'll feel there is little you can't accomplish, and you will be right. Because Mercury joins the Sun in Aries on the 16th it's a lucky time for paperwork, legal matters, travelling and making minor adjustments to all your plans. New people you meet will be informative and educational but not necessarily romantic.

From the emotional viewpoint you need to be extremely careful up until the 22nd, because there's a strong possibility of you becoming involved with members of the opposite sex whose company may require a certain amount of secrecy, perhaps because one or other of you have somebody else tucked away in the background. Now, Aries, you're such an open person you're really not fitted to any kind of intrigue, although the thought does tend to titillate you! If you've a special person in your life you truly value, you'll stick to the straight and narrow; if not, it might be a good idea to make a clean break before you launch into yet another torrid affair.

Financially, you seem to be beavering around in the background, perhaps chasing up money, until the 22nd, but without making a great deal of progress. Why not save yourself the aggravation and wait until Venus enters your sign on the 22nd when you'll certainly be receiving the green light from the stars to push ahead in all areas including financial. You'll have so much charm later in the month that nobody can resist you at work, within the family or where romance is concerned. The big question is; have you enough patience to wait for this date before rushing headlong into life? The answer to this is questionable but do your best, you can do no more.

Because your ruling planet, Mars, is in retrograde movement it will draw back into the sign of Virgo on the 8th and so the pace is likely to hot up quite considerably where work is concerned. Naturally, as an energetic fire sign, this won't phase you, but even so you can overdo it, particularly at this time. See what you can do to pace yourself on the working front because there's so much fun to be had in other areas; you don't want to miss out because that would really upset you. Now for a look at the state of the Moon.

The New Moon occurs on the 9th in the watery sign of Pisces. You may learn of some information or perhaps a secret which you can use in order to push ahead with your ambitions at a later date. You may also discover that your feelings towards somebody else are changing and becoming a good deal deeper; this may surprise you but at least you're not going to be bored. As always, New Moons can be used for making important decisions or actions and this one is no exception. So be a little more daring around this period.

The Full Moon occurs on the 24th in your opposite sign of Libra. Oh dear! If you have a relationship which is in trouble then it could very well come to a grinding halt around this time and, unless you want this to happen, you'll need to do some fast thinking and a quick rescue job. On the other hand, of course, it may be that the relationship has run its course and you're about ready to throw in the towel. Everybody who is closest to you needs to be treated with a little more respect and sensitivity around this time in order to avoid any kind of upset. As always, Full Moons can be used for making plans but are not ideal for leaping into action.

APRIL

With the Sun in your sign up until 20 April, this is certainly one period of the year when you must be ready to open your arms to all opportunities to expand your life on all levels. It's an especially lucky period for those in positions of authority or power and great for the Arian who is trying to set up a new business, something the Ram simply can't resist and frequently does again and again until eventually succeeding. Your confidence knows no bounds but it might be a good idea to tone yourself down a little, particularly when dealing with the more timid members of the human race, because as you wave your arms around, shouting at the top of your voice, some of us can find it all a little too much and may even resort to earplugs. Even so, this is just the time for pushing ahead with everything that is important to you in all areas; you've solar power coming out of your ears and it's relatively easy for you to persuade other people around to your way of thinking, so, regardless of your job push ahead; let other people in on your plans and you should be able to make this a highly successful time.

Also, during the first couple of weeks, Venus will be squatting in your Sign with the Sun, which is good news for those involved in a professional partnership or the arts. The salesperson won't be doing too badly either because you certainly have a platinum-plated tongue at this time and can talk yourself into and out of situations in record time. Nobody can resist you so order books should be full.

Later in the month, the Sun and Venus will be moving into the cash area of life and your attitude to this 'necessary evil' changes completely. Just for once you'll be reluctant to spend and may even become something of a hoarder. It's certainly a great time for the collector who will be picking up some bargains. A professional buyer will be doing well, too, and your boss is sure to have a big smile on his or her face. Yes, there's no doubt about it, Aries, during the latter part of this month you won't be doing anything for nothing; and there's no point in other people expecting any kind of favour, time is money, that's your motto and you'll be sticking to it like glue.

Because Mercury is also sailing through the cash area of life, many of you will be gaining through travel, new contacts, legal affairs and also paperwork of all descriptions. You'll be picking up useful little tips from people you meet casually and these will be giving you plenty of food for thought. Money that is owed to you is likely to come rolling in up until the 15th, while Venus coasts along through your Sign. If you're doing any kind of negotiating, you're sure to come out on top, so push ahead with confidence, Aries, although it is unlikely you could progress in any other way!

Emotionally, those softer feelings of yours are easily touched during the first two weeks, so there's a strong possibility of many of you falling in love at this time. This new relationship is unlikely to be a 'flash in the pan', it's sure to be deep and meaningful and could really be going places in the future. If you're already in a relationship, you may be prepared to take it a step further, and those Rams who decide to become engaged or married during the first two weeks of this month have certainly picked the ideal time, because happiness is all but guaranteed.

Healthwise, your ruling planet, Mars, continues to squat in the earthy sign of Virgo so the biggest danger to health is overwork, but when isn't it? Do make sure that you set aside some time for real relaxation – a period when you can let the whole world drift away because in this way you will replenish and renew yourself. Mind you, such a placing can also cause a certain amount of aggravation amongst the workforce and, although you may not be directly involved, somehow the atmosphere is sure to affect you; see what you can do to act the role of peacemaker, a title not normally associated with your Sign but on temporary loan to you during this month.

There seems to be a great deal going for you this month, Aries, and it's imperative to channel your energy constructively to make the most of all opportunities which come your way. Refer to the *Daily Guides* as you'll find them invaluable when it comes to avoiding trouble or making the most of opportunities. Now for a look at the state of the Moon.

The New Moon occurs on the 7th and, wouldn't you know it, it's in your own sign. This is a clear indication then that you're beginning a minor new cycle in life and one that is filling you full of excitement. It's a time, too, when you can afford to push out into life confidently, in the knowledge that you can get your own way, as long as you use your charm. A new possession may delight you, or if you're fancy-free a new love sends the adrenalin pounding through your veins. Any way you look at it, this is likely to be a happy time for you.

The Full Moon occurs on the 22nd in the watery sign of Scorpio; if ever there was a pointer from the stars for you to observe all rules and regulations, this is it. It doesn't matter whether we're talking about using equipment correctly at work or obeying traffic rules and regulations; if you rush headlong into life without using at least one grey cell, I'm afraid you could be making life difficult for yourself. Luckily, at least this Full Moon, like any other, can be used for making plans but not acting on them. No matter how impatient you grow, use your will-power to control yourself, at least until this phase has passed, then you can push out into life once more in your usual energetic and dynamic fashion.

MAY

May is one of those rare months when you turn a great deal of your attention over to the financial side of life, due to the fact that the Sun is squatting in the sign of Taurus up until the 22nd. This is most certainly excellent news for those of you involved in the financial professions, whether it be as banker, collector, financier or even simply if you want to save your money, for reasons best known to yourself. If you can't manage to put a little cash by during this period then there's no hope for you, Aries, so get out that one sensible grey cell and give it a great deal of exercise, because you'll be glad you did.

Mercury, fortunately, resumes direct movement on the 8th and is squatting in the earth sign of Taurus, once more in the cash area of life. When it comes to signing important financial documents, wait until the second week because then they are guaranteed to bring you success in the future. If you sign on the dotted line before this time, you'll be storing up unnecessary aggravation for yourself which, quite frankly, you'll want to avoid. There seems to be a great deal of communication on the telephone where money matters are concerned. Perhaps you're chasing money that's owed or trying to get together some kind of deal. Either way you should be in luck.

From the 22nd onwards, the Sun will have moved into the sign of Gemini. Workwise this is certainly a great time for those of you involved in buying, selling, the media, sales or any kind of communication, because you'll be able to find the right phrase at the right time, which will impress other people. Should any chance crop up for you to travel for the sake of professional duties, grab it with both hands because it will most certainly be lucky for you.

Venus' move into Gemini on the 11th has various interpretations. Firstly, there'll be a tendency for you to spend on minor luxuries, but the important word here is 'minor' and not major. It's a time, too, when you'll be able to express yourself with more charm and courtesy, which will make an impression on other people and, because of this, brief encounters will be innumerable during this period. Yes, Aries, you're certainly about to be spoiled for choice, but if you've already got a partner you'll need to fight like the devil to control temptation. You enjoy the hint of excitement and, as a Ram, how can you possibly resist any kind of challenge? The answer to this is, with a great deal of will-power, that is if you want to hang on to your current partner anyway. Naturally the choice as always is yours.

Luckily, your ruling planet, Mars, has finally decided to resume direct movement, so if you have experienced the feeling of taking one step forward and fifty backwards, this tendency will now come to an end and you will find you are gradually moving towards your ambitions, no matter what they might be. Mind you, Neptune is now in retrograde movement, so on the working front confusion and mystery may crop up from time to time and, unless it directly affects you, it would be a good idea to get on with your own business and let other people sort out their own dramas. Certainly May seems to be a time full of action and incident and there's nothing you like better than to be kept busy, let's face it. Now for a look at the state of the Moon.

The New Moon occurs on the 6th in the earthy sign of Taurus, which is, of course, the financial area of your life. So, for some lucky Rams, there's a strong possibility of a fresh source of income; for others there may be a delightful present or an exciting new purchase which you can't wait to show off to other people. All important financial moves should be centred around this time because you really can't fail, all you have to do is believe it. As always, New Moons can be used for starting anything new whether it's a relationship, a project or a leisure-time activity.

The Full Moon occurs on the 22nd in the fiery sign of Sagittarius, so this is definitely a time to be careful when in the company of those who come from different countries, as you will easily upset them. Furthermore, if it is necessary for you to travel any distance, cancel where possible, otherwise double, treble and even quadruple your attention to all arrangements, connections and times of flights, or you'll find yourself sitting around on your suitcase, gnawing your fingernails down to the bone in frustration, and it's so easy to avoid. As always, Full Moons are excellent for laying down plans but certainly not the best time in the world for leaping into action, so control the impulsive side to your character if you possibly can. See what you can do.

JUNE

The Sun will be pottering along in the sign of Gemini, accompanied by Mercury, up until the 21st, and so you'll be finding lots of small excuses for taking short trips; it will be hard for you to sit still and behave yourself for any length of time; you need to be constantly on the go, not just mentally but physically too.

The lucky professions up until the 21st continue to be those connected with advertising, sales, media and jobs where you need to rely on good ideas and inspiration. You'll find it unusually difficult to sit still for any length of time, even on the working front, and will be finding excuses to pop out for half-an-hour here and half-an-hour there. Self-expression continues to flow more easily up until the 23rd, so if you need to be persuasive on a professional front, particularly at negotiations or meetings, you'd be hard put to fail. Yes, Aries, you're certainly making a big impression during this period.

From the 21st onwards the Sun will be moving into the watery sign of Cancer when it meets up with Venus. During the last few days of the month, it is those of you who work in connection with property, and that includes

the building industry, electricians and plumbers who will
be doing well. For other airy Rams, there'll be a strong
urge to improve your surroundings and it certainly looks
as if money is going to be spent on decoration; naturally
you'll choose the best. Have you asked yourself if you
can afford it? For some of you, instead of beautifying your
surroundings, you may develop a strong need for company
at home and, if you have a special occasion to celebrate,
such as a birthday or an engagement, rest assured it will go
with a swing and everybody will be impressed. Well, let's
face it, Aries, apart from Leo, you're one of the Zodiac's
best when it comes to being a host or hostess, when you
really put your mind to it.

If you're a family person, at least relatives will have little
to grumble about during this month because they seem to
be getting a great deal of attention. Perhaps this is due to
a guilty conscience? I wouldn't be at all surprised. Still, as
long as they are happy that's something. Whilst talking
about families, you may discover that a relative has a
really good money-spinning idea, so sit down and listen
before you dismiss them with a wave of your impatient
hand. After all, they are allowed their opinion just as you
are allowed yours. Let's get some sense of justice here.

Your ruling planet, Mars, will be moving into your
opposite sign of Libra on the 19th; this has both its
positive and negative influences. Let's take the negative
first of all. There's likely to be quite a lot of tension
in your relationships with those who mean the most
to you and flare-ups occur over practically nothing, so
someone will need to keep a sense of proportion and, quite
frankly, it might just as well be you. On the other hand,
if you're fancy-free, this placing could suggest several new
hormone-churning, physical relationships. Hopefully you
don't have a partner, because you're not the most discreet
of people, are you, Aries? Still, if you're fancy-free, there
is no reason at all why you shouldn't indulge yourself,
always providing, of course, that you use the necessary

precautions. It doesn't pay to take chances; being an impulsive Arian is no excuse, believe me! However, with any luck, sensible Saturn coasting through your Sign may just help you to stop and think before you do something rash, which you would live to regret.

Certainly, there is a lot for you to think about during this month; always remember stars impel, they do not compel, so read the *Daily Guides* in order to make the most of each and every day. Now for a look at the state of the Moon.

The New Moon occurs on the 5th in the air sign of Gemini; this will certainly be providing a healthy jolt to those grey cells; you'll be bursting full of good ideas and so need to keep pen and paper handy, because they could fly in one ear and out the other, something you would certainly regret. It's a period when you'll want to keep on the go and, in the process of dashing through life, you'll be making new contacts who will, at a later date, become close friends. Communications are emphasized at this time too, so all important phone calls should be centred around this period of the month for maximum effect; good for meetings and negotiations too. As always with New Moons you can afford to keep a higher profile and be your usual daring self, because life will be smiling sweetly down upon you.

The Full Moon occurs on the 20th in the fiery sign of Sagittarius. Oh dear! I hope you're not taking any kind of test or examination, or are thinking of travelling because, if you are, things could become horribly confused. Should this be unavoidable, double-check your arrangements every step along the way, not just once, not just twice, but as many times as you can. Better still, where possible, cancel until a luckier time. Full Moons can be a real pain making life twice as difficult as it already is. Still, as always, they are great for making plans for the future and it looks as if you'll be making some pretty ambitious ones during this particular month, although hopefully you won't act on them for the time being.

JULY

Because the Sun will be squatting in the watery sign of Cancer up until the 23rd the emphasis continues to be on family and home life. Many of you may be considering moving from one district to another, others may be changing flatmates and still other Rams moving in with a special love. Workwise, the building industry and all its allied trades continues to thrive, so hopefully you're involved in this direction. If you're thinking of buying a house or a flat, move as early in the month as is possible because you should be able to pick one up at a reasonable price.

From the 23rd onwards, the Sun will have moved into the fiery sign of Leo which will certainly be helpful to those of you involved in show business, with children, animals, creativity and the arts in general. Yes, that imagination will be taking flight, and certainly you'll be impressing prospective clients or even bosses.

Whilst at the beginning of the month you decide to socialize at home, for one reason or another after the 23rd, you break out into the world in your usual dramatic fashion. All glamorous occasions will appeal; you'll want to go to glitzy parties, first nights and in general keep a high profile. Do make sure, though, that you don't come across as being a little too 'pushy', because you could lose potential contacts and friends if you're not careful.

With Mercury in the fiery sign of Leo, many of you will be taking on new intellectual pastimes; this is very unlike you because basically Aries is a physical sign, but, just for once, you have decided to exercise the grey matter between your ears, and may want to learn about the occult, take up backgammon or engage in some other form of mental activity. You may even sit still long enough to read a book or at least a chapter. If you are a parent, children will be providing you with a tremendous amount of pleasure and joy at this time; maybe they have found some success of their own and you're puffing up with pride.

Venus will be situated in Leo up until the 24th, again very helpful for the artistic, but also a great shot in the arm for your social life. You'll need to keep a diary handy or you may find yourself double-booked and you know how you hate to miss out on anything.

Emotionally, you're at your most flirtatious, so hopefully you're fancy-free because otherwise there are likely to be one or two heart-stopping moments for your partner. As an Aries you love a challenge and, even though you may be married, you can't help but reassure yourself that you are as attractive as you once were, by chasing a tempting proposition simply for the sake of getting the satisfaction of a favourable response. This is a dangerous game to play, Aries, which, of course, only makes it all the more exciting for you. Luckily, you begin to see common sense from the 24th onwards, when you decide to turn your attention to improving your health in some way, by perhaps joining a gym or engaging in some other sporting endeavour. Your relationship with your workmates will be improving in leaps and bounds, too, and you don't seem to have an ulterior motive for a change. There may be an exchange of ideas and/or the starting of a new exciting project, which will set the adrenalin flowing through your veins.

Cashwise, up until the 24th, there may be a strong tendency for you to speculate or gamble in some way; if you must, do refer to the *Daily Guides* and find a time when Venus is well aspected, because otherwise you could find yourself seriously out of pocket.

Your ruling planet, Mars, continues to coast along through your opposite sign of Libra and temporarily you could take on some of the characteristics of this sign, becoming more fair-minded, developing a stronger sense of justice and not becoming quite so worked up over little inconveniences. Yes, your sense of fair play certainly seems to be increasing and this will be impressing those around you. Mind you, the old hormones are still leaping up and down and so it won't take much to set you off;

glimpsing a shapely leg or a pair of broad shoulders finds
you coming out in a hot sweat. This, of course, can be fun
if you happen to be fancy-free, but you're flirting with
danger, my Aries friend, if you happen to have a partner
who you seriously care about. You must weigh up the
pros and cons and decide whether or not the gamble is
worthwhile; only you can make that decision.

Saturn continues to coast along through your sign,
taking its time, and, with any luck, this will be increasing
the practical and common sense side to your character,
which is often sadly lacking. You'll be more prepared to
take on responsibility, not only for your own actions, but
for other people's too, and indirectly, at some point in the
future, this could lead to a promotion. All in all then, July
certainly seems to be packed full of action, so hopefully
you'll make the most of it. Now for a look at the state of
the Moon.

The New Moon this month occurs on the 4th, in the
watery sign of Cancer. As the area of your chart devoted
to property and family, it could, of course, suggest a
celebration or a party at home, in which case you'll
be having the time of your life. On the other hand, it
might denote a new beginning, perhaps news of a birth,
engagement or even a wedding, certainly some excuse to
have fun and celebrate, as if you ever need one.

The Full Moon occurs on the 20th, in the sign of
Capricorn, which is the zenith of your chart. Luckily,
it's a Sunday, because otherwise you might be strongly
tempted to tell your boss exactly what to do with the job
and then you may find yourself out on the street. Still, we
have to remember that some Arians do work on Sundays
and if you are one of these unfortunates, try to keep your
hot temper under control because otherwise there could be
unpleasant repercussions at a later date. The last thing you
need to do at this time is to mix business with pleasure,
because you're likely to be at loggerheads with colleagues
and this could ruin the atmosphere on the working front.

As always, Full Moons are a great time for giving your plans an airing, getting other people's reactions to them, but not for implementing them for the time being.

AUGUST

The majority of this month is going to be very similar to the fun and games that were going on in late July, mainly because the Sun continues to be in the fire sign of Leo up until the 23rd. Naturally, by now, you may realize this is a part of your chart devoted to pleasure, children, flighty romance, creativity and animals. So, should you work in any of these fields, you're bound to have a successful time. If not, it's likely that your social calendar is full to bursting point and you're going to be hard put to fulfil all those obligations; however, if anyone can do it, you can Aries, certainly you'll be giving it your best shot, that's for sure.

Once the Sun moves out of Leo on the 23rd and into the earthy sign of Virgo it's Rams who are employed in the service industries who will suddenly find themselves in great demand. On the other hand, it may be that you need to hire somebody else's talents and, if so, you'll certainly be getting good value for money.

Healthwise, Mercury in Virgo could make you a little jittery, particularly on the working front where there's a strong possibility that you could overdo it. Promise yourself that you'll get in at least a couple of early nights and you should remain hale and hearty, but if you insist on working all day and playing all night, I'm afraid you could very well finish up on the sick-list and you'll have nobody to blame but your good self. To make matters worse, Venus will be in Virgo up until the 18th, a planet which encourages excesses in all their many forms, so there is a strong possibility that you are going to be suffering from at least one hangover this month and maybe even more, unless you exercise a little self-control; see what you can do!

Financially, Venus' placing in Libra from the 18th onwards suggests that other people are keen to listen to your plans and maybe even supply some backing. Those involved in professional partnerships should certainly be doing well as should those who rely heavily on their contacts, because this is definitely one month when it's who you know and not what you know which will help to swell your bank balance.

Of course, with Venus and Mars squatting in the sign of Libra, the emphasis is bound to be on the intensely personal side of life. And, this is one period in the year when, if you want to make an important commitment, you can feel free to do so in the knowledge you are doing the right thing. On the other hand, if you're fancy-free, August will be providing you with many opportunities for falling in love, or falling in lust or, with any luck, both. Yes, you certainly must be looking your best, because other people are falling over themselves to make contact with you and in the nicest possible way too.

Fortunately, after a protracted period in retrograde movement, Pluto finally decides to see common sense and resume direct motion on the 13th, which is certainly going to make life a great deal easier for those of you who are either studying or travel for a living. If life has been full of turbulence and transformation, you can now begin to look forward to a much more tranquil and less complicated life.

Mind you, with Neptune continuing its retrograde action for a little longer, it wouldn't be a good idea to get involved with gossip on the working front, because you may be tempted to elaborate a little and this could backfire on you at a later date. Ignore all rumours and gossip; people are simply trying to liven up their boring day by inventing little stories, and the last thing you should do is to take them seriously. Now for a look at the state of the Moon.

This month the New Moon occurs in the fiery sign of Leo, on the 3rd, which suggests an exciting social occasion that you may be looking forward to. On the other hand, it could very well provide you with a new romance or the chance to take part in something creative. If you are a parent, this is the best possible time for getting through to your children, if you've been out of touch recently. As always, New Moons are a time for keeping in the thick of the action, and there's certainly plenty of it around at this time.

The Full Moon occurs on the 18th in the air sign of Aquarius. Be a little careful around this period, Aries, because there is a distinct possibility that unwittingly you may upset a friend and then bang goes a relationship which you cherish a great deal, although you may not realize it until it has come to an end. Avoid airing your opinions to close friends unless they are asked for; it won't take much to put you out of favour around the Full Moon, so try to bear this in mind.

As always, this is a great time for making plans but certainly not one for keeping a high profile or putting plans into action. There's no reason at all, of course, why you can't discuss your plans with those closest to you; they may be able to give you a fresh slant on them or may even point out something that you have completely overlooked. If so, don't become angry, your ego can be too sensitive on occasions, you know.

SEPTEMBER

Like it or not, Aries, there comes a point in any year when it's definitely a case of 'nose to the grindstone' and I'm afraid this is it, well, up until the 23rd anyway. You need to control the ambitious side of your character and be more prepared to be thorough in everything you turn your attention to, because mistakes are easily made. A positive way of looking at this is that if you can stick to routine, this surely leaves you freer to enjoy yourself in other areas of life, which can be no bad thing. Mind you, the exception to this are the Arians involved in the service industries, the medical profession or even charity work. If this applies to you, it's going to be a hectic time but one which you will find extremely stimulating as well as rewarding. However, with Mercury in retrograde movement up until the 10th, whatever you do, avoid signing important documents; take care on all kinds of trips and, if you have to travel long-distance, treble and quadruple your checks on times of arrival, connections and all related details.

Healthwise, you may find yourself becoming far more easily tired than is usually the case, certainly within the first ten days of the month anyway. So, if you can persuade yourself to pace work at a sensible level, you'll avoid this little pitfall, and it won't become necessary for you to cancel romantic dates or even socializing, which is something you'd be loth to do. From the 23rd onwards, the fiery Sun will be moving into your opposite sign of Libra, which is certainly good news for those of you in professional partnerships, the Arians who act on behalf of other people, such as agents, managers or representatives and in general, for all Rams, late in the month is a time for listening to the ideas of other people instead of ramming your own down their poor unwilling throats.

Venus will be squatting in your opposite sign of Libra up until the 12th, throwing a peaceful and rosy glow over all existing relationships, and bringing opportunities for romance for the fancy-free. Socially, you are likely to be rushed off your feet during the first couple of weeks, but don't be surprised if the phone goes horribly quiet after this. In truth, this can be no bad thing because even you need to rest up sometimes and, if you're not going to do it voluntarily, it's just as well other people have suddenly become unsociable, so you have to spend some time alone. From the 12th onwards, Venus moves into the watery sign of Scorpio where it meets up with sexy Mars. Certainly, it's going to be a hectic time for those of you involved with big institutions like banks, banking and insurance and the Stock Exchange. Mind you, there is another side to this coin because Mars can be extremely sexy in this watery sign of Scorpio. In fact, there could be moments when you can think of little else; your friends could take to handcuffing their partners to their sides, because they'll sense your mood after only one quick glance at you.

September certainly isn't a month for flaunting the law or ticking off your bank manager and telling him or her how to run the business; you could make some powerful enemies and live to regret it at a later date. Maybe you've done this before and got away with it, but I'm afraid that just simply won't be the case during September, so watch yourself. Now for a look at the state of the Moon.

The New Moon occurs on the 1st in the earthy sign of Virgo, so it looks as if there's going to be plenty of news amongst your colleagues, maybe even some opportunities through listening to what they have to say, so don't dismiss them before they've had a chance to open their mouths. This is also a good time for getting health or dental check-ups; the news will be good so you needn't worry. A good time, too, for bargain hunting; you could strike gold in some way. As always, try to keep a high profile during a New Moon because you never know what or who you may bump into.

The Full Moon occurs in the watery sign of Pisces on the 16th, this is the secretive part of your birth chart and so this is not particularly good news, mainly because you may be feeling insecure and keeping your fears and worries to yourself. This is not a healthy way to carry on; surely there must be someone in your circle, or in your family, you can trust, and, if so, a little outpouring of all of this stress can do you the world of good; so see what you can do. As always, of course, Full Moons are a great time for putting the finishing touches to work or for making plans for the future, and this one is no exception.

OCTOBER

With the Sun and Mercury situated in the air sign of Libra, during most of the month, this is certainly a time when the stars are suggesting, even insisting, that you co-operate more with other people. Certainly, if you work in a professional partnership or on behalf of other people, such as being a representative, an agent or manager, you're in for a successful time. However, this is not a period for being too self-sufficient, Aries; like it or not, you have to consider the wants and needs of other people on the working front and, if necessary, reach some kind of 'compromise', a word which you absolutely hate.

From the 23rd onwards, the Sun will be moving into the watery sign of Scorpio, which is certainly good news for those of you who work in big institutions such as banks, insurance and the Stock Exchange; it is good, too, for Arians who need to deal with such people. However, you may be unduly concerned about somebody else's ability to keep their end up where household expenses are concerned. Maybe a flatmate has hit a bad period or somebody is out of work, either way you mustn't give in to the temptation to soldier on alone just in order to show everybody how big and strong you really are, because this will have a detrimental effect not only on your health but also on your bank account. So, confront this situation as quickly as you can, so that you know exactly what you're up against. If you've found yourself experiencing a run-in with officials, whether it be the taxman or anybody else, the last week of the month is an ideal time for arranging meetings, because you'll find people much more reasonable and approachable at this time.

Mercury's placing in your opposite sign of Libra between the 2nd and the 19th is likely to be bringing a good deal more contact with people. This may not necessarily be of a sexual or emotional nature, rather it seems that you have found several people with whom you have a great deal in common and you're forging strong bonds, or perhaps even joining forces in some way.

Your ruling planet, Mars, will be squatting in the fiery sign of Sagittarius for the entire month, so you could be temporarily taking on some of the characteristics of this sign, becoming more of a daredevil, travel-conscious and even considering taking on a fresh line of study. Those of you who have decided to take a short break will certainly find travel enjoyable and uncomplicated.

Emotionally, it's those strange names and exotic places which will hold strong appeal for you throughout October. Yes, you definitely have a taste for those from completely different backgrounds than yourself which could prove to be a learning experience and therefore no bad thing. However, don't start listening for wedding bells too soon because relationships are likely to be fairly short-lived, if exciting, whilst they're on the go.

If you're a Ram taking any kind of test or examination, you couldn't have picked a better time. Whether it's a driving test, or some other kind of examination, you should do well, providing you don't get over-confident. Yours is not a Sign that thinks too much about further education. However, during October, something may occur which makes you realize that it might be a good idea to take a fresh course of learning; if so, don't simply think about it, do something practical, because you'll be glad you did at a much later date. Any opportunities to visit different environments, or even travel abroad, should be snapped up without further delay because this is sure to be lucky for you.

Cashwise, once more, there's an exotic feel about the month. Money seems to be coming through those who live or work abroad, or perhaps those from abroad who live in this country. It's certainly worthwhile keeping a keen ear open for an unusual accent, financially as well as romantically.

Finally, Neptune has decided to resume forward movement and so the mysterious atmosphere which may have lurked in your work surroundings slowly disappears. Others, there, are less inclined to gossip and make heavy weather of relatively straightforward jobs; this appeals to your Arian nature, which, basically, is fairly uncomplicated, certainly where ambitions are concerned.

With the majority of the planets above the horizon, this month, certainly it's a time which should appeal to the adventurous side of your character, because it's one when you should be reaching out into life, seeking out new experiences, fresh faces and generally giving free rein to the adventurer within. Do that and you'll be making the most out of this particular month. Now for a look at the state of the Moon.

The New Moon occurs on the 1st of the month in your opposite sign of Libra, so there is more than just a hint that you may be making a new relationship, be it professional or personal. If you have been stuck in a relationship and things have become a little boring or stale, this is the time for introducing a little excitement; so put on your thinking cap. On the other hand, if you happen to be fancy-free, it's a time for keeping a high profile because you'll be attracting the opposite sex to you in droves. You're looking good and feeling good, so go for it, Aries. As always, New Moons can be used for making fresh starts in any area of life you choose.

The Full Moon occurs on the 16th in your own sign, a clear suggestion that you seem to be coming to the end of a minor cycle, in some way, and, although you may not believe it at the moment, in the very near future you'll realize this is the best possible outcome. You may be feeling a little insecure, but if you keep company with people who make you laugh, there's no reason why you shouldn't enjoy the day. As always, it's a good time for making plans but not one for acting.

Lastly, we are blessed with a second New Moon, this month, and it occurs on 31 October in the watery sign of Scorpio. This may be resurrecting old feelings for somebody you were once close to; you're in something of a nostalgic frame of mind, very rare for an Arian but nevertheless quite enjoyable, because you could be visiting a place you haven't been to for some time. Emotions are easily stirred and the relationship which began fairly casually seems to be gathering momentum. A nice way to end any month. As always, try to keep a high profile during a New Moon and be prepared to give full rein to that adventurous side of your character.

NOVEMBER

With the Sun continuing in the watery sign of Scorpio, the emphasis is still firmly placed on jobs which are connected with high finance, banking, insurance and related areas. If you need to raise some capital for one of your brilliant ideas, pick a good time within the *Daily Guides* and act; don't simply think about it.

From the 22nd onwards, the Sun will be moving into the fiery sign of Sagittarius, which is good news for the Rams who work in higher education, the law and travel affairs. It's a good time, too, for the Ram who wants to take a short break, and probably deserves it anyway. Besides, you're in desperate need for a little bit of an adventure and some fresh faces, so this is the ideal time to get cracking because, whether we like it or not, Christmas and New Year are looming over the horizon and then there'll be little chance for you to escape the daily grind.

Mercury in Sagittarius makes it a good time to sign any kind of contract; you can afford to do so in the knowledge that it will help to enrich you in some way; if not right now, then in the future. All paperwork and documents will be of great importance, so if you've any doubt about them, for heaven's sake, take them to an expert for an explation before you add your signature.

At the moment, you seem to be neglecting the more domestic side of life; you're not exactly a home body at the best of times, but you do seem to be taking this to extreme and so, if you're not careful, members of your family will soon start to object in no uncertain fashion. Why not do yourself a favour, get on the phone and have a long chat with them.

During November, both Venus and your ruling planet, Mars, will be coasting along at the zenith of your chart in the gritty sign of Capricorn. Because Mars is your ruling planet, you could temporarily take on some of the characteristics of this planet, becoming more grounded, practical and even down-to-earth. Whatever next? The workload is likely to be heavy but you seem to be wallowing in all the action that seems to be whizzing around your ears. The placing of Venus in Capricorn will certainly be useful to those of you who work in artistic jobs and, regardless of your own sex, you'll find women extremely helpful to you.

Cashwise, don't expect any added bonuses; you're going to be working hard and will be well rewarded in the future, so relax. When socializing with workmates, as I think you'll be doing quite a lot this month, try to avoid socializing with those who have expensive tastes, because you're so easily led astray.

Emotionally, with Venus and Mars in Capricorn, there's likely to be some kind of entanglement with the opposite sex in connection with your job. If you already have a partner, it looks as if you're in for a troublesome month, or certainly a confusing one, but, of course, if you are fancy-free, you can afford to indulge yourself. However, always remember that when an affair is over with a colleague you're still involved with them, on one level. Still, with any luck perhaps you won't want to exclude the person from your life.

Healthwise, despite the hard work, the heavy social commitments and the other hundred and one things you seem to have to worry about, you manage to stay ridiculously healthy, and, if you want to stay that way, at least get in one or two early nights because it can only do you the power of good. After all, if you're really going to be in such demand with the opposite sex, you certainly want to have a wet nose and a shiny coat, otherwise they may be attracted to others, which would never do – too much of a blow to the ego!

The planets continue to cluster around the top of your solar chart and so family matters are put on the back-burner for the time being; you're thinking big and talking big, but whatever you do don't boast, because your words could come home to roost at a later date. November seems to be a month when you're living life to the fullest extent and, in your book, that's the only way to exist and you're probably right. Nevertheless, Aries, you are human, so try to be a little kinder to your body, because we've a hectic time ahead of us just over the horizon and you want to be ready to make the most of that too; you hate to miss out. Now for a look at the state of the Moon.

This month the Full Moon occurs on the 14th in the gritty sign of Taurus, which, unfortunately for you, happens to be the cash area of life as well as representing your possessions. Look after your valuables, they could easily go astray or may be lifted by light fingers. Keep them in a safe place at home and, in that way, you may be able to minimize any difficulties. Because this particular Full Moon has such a financial feel about it, it wouldn't be a good idea to push your luck, for example, with gambling, or even asking for a raise; this would be committing financial suicide. As always, Full Moons should be used for making plans but certainly not for leaping into impulsive action because that'll only get you in trouble.

The New Moon occurs on the 30th, in the fiery sign of Sagittarius so, if you have any connections abroad you will most certainly be hearing from them in the very near future. And, if you are thinking of changing your image or improving your mind, don't just think about it, take some constructive action, because this will be an ideal time for doing just that. There'll be new people entering your life too, probably from completely different backgrounds from yourself and you'll find them fascinating, so much so that a romance may even develop, although don't expect it to last for any length of time. As always, New Moons are times when you should keep in the thick of the action and not be afraid to air some of your secret desires, wishes or plans, because you'll find a warm welcome waiting for them. Certainly, then, November looks to be the kind of month you can really get your teeth into.

DECEMBER

Up until the 22nd of the month, the Sun will be squatting in the fiery sign of Sagittarius, again throwing the emphasis on higher education, legal matters and foreign affairs. So, if you work in these areas of life, you're sure to be doing very well for yourself. After the 22nd, the Sun will be moving to the zenith of your chart and, ideally, you should be starting one of the most ambitious parts of your year, but the festive period is sure to interfere. Never mind, there's a strong likelihood that you'll be mixing business with pleasure a great deal and, in doing so, you may be able to put forward your ideas and suggestions on a social level, which is often more acceptable than doing so in a more formal fashion.

You need to take care that loved ones at home aren't being serious neglected; because you've been so busy with external interests, you've had little time for your personal life and somebody is becoming seriously discontented right now. Venus will be situated in Capricorn up until the 12th, so clearly you're mixing business with pleasure a great deal and flirting like crazy. It's a good time for the creative Ram; though it is a little late in the year, it's never too late to present your ideas to other people, even if you can't put them into action until next year.

Once Venus moves into Aquarius on the 12th, there's a rosy glow over teamwork, friends, acquaintances and contacts and, if this is an important side of your job, you'll be doing very well for yourself. Emotionally, if you are fancy-free, during the early part of the month you may meet people, through your job, and then later on through friends who could be trying to pay you off. Come on, Aries, if you're lonely, shelve that pride and go along with their ideas and suggestions; after all, what have you got to lose, just a couple of hours of your time, that's not too much to ask, surely?

Cashwise, because your money planet, Venus, is squatting in Aquarius, that rather eccentric sign, you need to get yourself highly organized when it comes to buying Christmas presents, because there'll be a tendency for you to suddenly splurge on items which are best described as 'shoddy'. Pace yourself in this direction; above all else make a list and stick to it like glue, we can't have you ending the year as you usually do – completely broke – because each year you swear you'll be more sensible, and each year, your good intentions fly out of the window. Why not try to stick to them during this particular year because then you'll end it feeling quite smug about yourself?

As for the festive period itself, well Aries, there's a strong tendency in you to allow other people to get on with it because, basically, you've got more important things to do, but ask yourself if this is strictly fair and, if you're honest, I think you'll agree the answer is 'no'. This year, then, try to pitch in with everybody else because, to your surprise, you may actually enjoy getting the family organized; you are, of course, a born leader. No doubt you can introduce a certain amount of fun into the usual party games because, with your vitality and enthusiasm, you can light up any room when you really want to; so make an effort over the festive period because loved ones will be forever grateful to you.

I think it's highly likely that when you look back on 1997, you'll realize that not only have you learnt a great deal, but that your progress has been fairly spectacular; let's hope it continues through 1998. Now for a look at the state of the Moon.

The Full Moon falls in the air sign of Gemini on the 14th. Be a little careful when in the company of friends, particularly if you are out drinking; it's likely that you could be indiscreet, blurting out a secret or perhaps a truth which was better left unsaid. Naturally, at this time of the year, it would be a shame to bring a long-standing relationship to an end, simply because you'd had one too many vodkas, or whatever your particular poison happens to be. Keep your feet on the ground and you should be able to prevent this from happening. Lastly, on no account should you take chances with drinking and driving on this day, because if you do you will most certainly get caught and that would get your Christmas off to a very bad start indeed.

The New Moon occurs on the 29th in the gritty sign of Capricorn, so it looks as if ambitions and thoughts of work return pretty quickly, once the festive period is over; you seem to be anxious to get back into the old routine, and, not surprisingly, this may not be well received by your loved ones. Ideally, you should try to control this mood when you're in their company. Of course, there's no reason why you shouldn't make the odd phone call if it satisfies this ambitious side of your character, but do make sure that you devote the rest of the year to the people who mean the most to you, and we're not talking about your boss or your supervisor. As always, New Moons are a great time for making fresh starts and because this one occurs at the zenith of your chart, it's likely you'll be working on a new ambition and will start making plans to turn it into a reality. Use other people as a sounding board and get their unbiased opinion; it won't influence you, of course, but it may give you the courage to turn your dream into a reality. Now refer to the *Daily Guides* for a more in-depth look.

Daily Guides

JANUARY

WEDNESDAY 1st   Career and cash affairs seem to be taking centre stage, mainly because there's so much activity at the zenith of your chart. Mind you, don't take anything for granted, because it's unlikely you'll be able to charm your way out of any difficulties. Because the Moon opposes you, it may seem as if it's you against the world; what you hear at work won't exactly be music to your ears, but you'll finally know where you stand with bosses and people in positions of authority.

THURSDAY 2nd   Your talent for putting your point of view across to those who have similar ambitions is very important now, because Mercury is in retrograde action, which means you're about to learn that the only hurdles to your progress are those you have created yourself. Once you realize this, you'll be much more optimistic about your chances and much better placed to influence the decisions of those you work with and those who control the purse-strings.

FRIDAY 3rd   Today, your ruling planet, Mars, moves into your opposite sign of Libra and so you will temporarily take on some of the characteristics of this sign, which means being more fair-minded, not quite so positive, and ready to listen to what other people have to say. Who knows, this could do wonders for your popularity? It looks as if the phone is going to be red-hot over the next few weeks, so maybe you should tone yourself down more often, if this is the result.

SATURDAY 4th   Because you're a fire sign, there are times when you can be a little too set on having your own way, but right now the stars are suggesting you become more open-minded, especially when faced with matters you know nothing about. Whatever you do, don't stoop to devious methods to win an argument or you may find yourself alone.

SUNDAY 5th   As your ruling planet, Mars, is moving through the sympathetic sign of Libra, this promises to be an encouraging and successful period. In fact, provided you don't lose your temper with a friend, neighbour or relative, this could turn out to be one of the most positive times of the entire month. You certainly have the support and backing of influential people, so it's simply a case of making better use of them.

MONDAY 6th   Today, you may be torn between the desire to broaden your horizons and the need to stabilize your cash position. Luckily, you're under no obligation to make an instant decision, so wait until the New Moon on the 9th for taking a plunge. Other aspects suggest that any inspirational ideas you have, mustn't be kept to yourself, so spread them around and watch them grow.

TUESDAY 7th   It looks as if some kind of choice will have to be made today, perhaps connected with your long-term ambitions, and money is sure to play a part in your decision. The stars signify that your lifestyle could easily be changed, but first you must stop fretting about the cost. Put what really interests you, as opposed to what pays the most, at the front of your plans and the offers will come in thick and fast. Your attitude to material things will change dramatically before the end of this month.

WEDNESDAY 8th   Jupiter's in a beautiful aspect with Neptune today, so you are most certainly at your most idealistic, creative and innovative. You're good company to spend time with too, because your sense of humour is witty but not unkind. Romance looks interesting this evening, although you seem to be stuck between two choices. What a lovely position to find yourself in!

THURSDAY 9th   Today is the New Moon; it occurs in the earthy sign of Capricorn, at the zenith of your chart, and so is a time for really stepping up your efforts where work is concerned, and putting your ambitions first, at least during this particular day. Any changes that are taking place in your working environment will be to your advantage; be patient for a little longer and everything will become so much clearer to you. So, time to keep a high profile, mind you, what else do you usually do?

FRIDAY 10th   Today, Venus moves to the zenith of your chart with practically every other planet and this throws a happy glow over the atmosphere there. It's a particularly good time if you happen to have a crush on a colleague, so why not speak up, there's no point in suffering in silence. It's a good time for creative work and for mixing business with pleasure. So, Aries, it looks as if the world is your oyster at this time, so open it up and grab the pearl.

SATURDAY 11th   Your ruling planet, Mars, is in a difficult aspect with Saturn today, so progress is going to be very much a case of stop and go. Some of you may also be feeling under the weather, perhaps due to a bout of the flu or a cold; you hate to be ill and are even more loth to coddle yourself, but it doesn't do any harm on occasions, and this is one of those times. If you can bear the thought of it, try to get in an early night, because in that way germs will soon leave you and find somebody else to pester. Think about it!

SUNDAY 12th You ruling planet, Mars, is in a difficult aspect with Mercury and this means you could say the wrong thing at the wrong time to the wrong person. Keep a civil tongue in your head and avoid criticisms for the time being, because they'll be destructive rather than constructive. Check appointments because you may have overlooked a meeting you are supposed to attend.

MONDAY 13th Luckily, Mercury finally decides to resume direct movement and so the recent muddles in connection with travel, paperwork, documents or even the law will soon become a thing of the past. The Moon is in the sign of Pisces today, so this will help to ginger up your imagination; if you need this where work is concerned, other people are sure to be impressed in a big way.

TUESDAY 14th Changes at work may be giving you a sleepless night, but there really is no reason to fret. In fact, what takes place soon will make you realize that even forced changes are working in your favour. Now isn't a time for clinging to old ideas, no matter how good you may think they are; make minor changes, these could enrich your life in ways you can't even imagine. Have a bit of faith in fate.

WEDNESDAY 15th If you're typical to your sign, you're usually the sort of person who wears your heart on your sleeve; this is true at the moment and, because of this, you're far more likely to make the first move when it comes to romance and emotion. With cash also taking a turn for the better, you have no excuse for sitting at home and watching the world go past your window.

THURSDAY 16th Today, anything you set your mind to will bring in positive and perhaps even lucrative results. Life really should be a lot of fun at present, although you must take care not to overdo things, as the emotional shake-up of recent aspects may take a little time to fade. Don't forget that being alone is not the same as being lonely.

FRIDAY 17th The Sun is in a wonderful aspect with Neptune and so you're at your most gentle, approachable and creative. There's a strong chance that you'll be asked to a rather glamorous occasion and this will send the blood pounding through your veins. Of course, your first thought will be 'what am I going to wear?', which gives you a wonderful excuse to spend unnecessary money, but under these circumstances I don't think anyone is going to be able to restrain you.

SATURDAY 18th Right now, professionally or person-ally, you can either charm or crash your way to success, the choice is yours. It may take a while for you to wake up to the fact that almost anything you touch can turn to gold, but even the most sceptical of Arians will have realized that this is a very special time in life and be able to sense that it's really a time to 'go for it'.

SUNDAY 19th Your ruling planet, Mars, lines up with exciting Uranus which certainly makes for a lively day. There's a certain magic and charisma about you which few can resist, so it's up to you to take advantage either emotionally or professionally. Don't hold back on your enterprising ideas; after all, how can they reach fruition if you haven't reached the starting post yet? This evening promises to be exciting too, so all in all this is one good 24-hour period.

MONDAY 20th Today, the Sun moves into the airy sign

of Aquarius. For you, this is the area of your chart devoted to friendship, acquaintances and team spirit. There's no point in you attempting to 'go it alone', in your usual Aries fashion, over the next couple of weeks; in fact, the more you co-operate with others the greater your success will be, on a professional, domestic and romantic front. The choice is, of course, yours but if you want to make the most of your luck, listen to the stars.

TUESDAY 21st The stars suggest that a financial wrangle can be resolved in your favour, or at the very least, make you understand there was nothing to get upset about in the first place, but what really counts, today, is that you don't let relationship difficulties distract you from more important matters. It also looks as if you will be involved in situations which raise your awareness, but you need a great deal of personal freedom if you are to make the most of what you discover.

WEDNESDAY 22nd Jupiter moves into the sign of Aquarius, the area of your chart devoted to your contacts and your friends and so, for the rest of the year, you could expect plenty of good news in this direction, as well as a great deal of support when it is most needed. If you work as part of a team, there's sure to be some breakthrough, at some point, which will allow you the opportunity to bask in the limelight.

THURSDAY 23rd Today is the Full Moon and it occurs in the fiery sign of Leo. This is not altogether the most pleasant of aspects because it seems that, if you work artistically you could suffer from some kind of mental block; on the other hand, it may be that a social or romantic occasion you were really looking forward to is about to be cancelled. Still, Aries, you're a resilient enough character and can bounce back from a great deal worse than this, can't you? Of course you can.

FRIDAY 24th   The Sun is lining up with Pluto, so you've an ideal 24-hour period for sorting out bureaucrats, officials and similar people. Yes, you've plenty of charm about you at this time and all you need is to do your homework so that the people who count, understand you're taking them seriously. Don't shut your eyes and hope that they'll go away, because naturally they won't, and you're far too much of a realist to expect them to.

SATURDAY 25th   Your ruling planet, Mars, is lining up with Pluto today, quite an explosive combination. You're definitely in the mood for making some bold transformations and changes; these are likely to surprise not only your family and loved ones but also those on the working front. You may find it extra hard to keep hold of your temper with people you meet casually who seem to you to be a little 'dim-witted'. This may not necessarily be so, Aries, so slow down a little as you stroll through life and you'll avoid hurting anybody's feelings.

SUNDAY 26th   Today, the Moon in Virgo is seriously encouraging you to be more receptive, open-minded and imaginative, even to the point of being a little dreamy. You're going to be changing some of your most deep-seated opinions too, much to the surprise of those closest to you. There's one thing about you, Aries, you're always ready to take on a new idea or a fresh outlook, particularly if it seems better than the one you have been sticking to simply out of habit, not a usual Arian pitfall but a human one.

MONDAY 27th   Whatever you do, don't waste too much of your time and your energy trying to decide whether you want to continue with a certain relationship or not, you'll only throw good time and energy after bad and to do so would upset that fiery nature of yours. It's far better to bring something to an end, if it seems to be having a negative effect on you and on your life. Remember you are a fire sign and negative situations are basically alien to your character.

TUESDAY 28th Because the Moon is in your opposite sign, you may be acting out of character and, for reasons known only to your good self, you may feel the need replan and rebuild your life right now. This is a time when you should concentrate more on strengthening your reputation and protecting everything you have gained to date. If you let anything, or anyone, of importance slip away you'll be kicking yourself from here until Christmas.

WEDNESDAY 29th Right now you'll take more interest in the whys and wherefores of situations and events instead of just taking things for granted. You may become unnecessarily involved in the affairs of colleagues and workmates but ideally you should let them sort out their own difficulties, because anything you try to do will only be seen as 'interfering', which of course isn't true; you're only trying to be of help but that's not the way your actions are being interpreted.

THURSDAY 30th Because the Moon is in your opposite sign of Libra, the area of your chart devoted to intensely personal relationships, romance is likely to be flirtatious and fun, and shouldn't be taken too seriously. If you're in a steady relationship, you need to be a little careful because your actions could be too easily misconstrued by other people, particularly your partner, whose imagination seems to be running riot at this time.

FRIDAY 31st Uranus is in a beautiful aspect with Pluto, so you can expect a great deal of change, perhaps turmoil, and movement in the friendship and contact area of life. Certainly, what occurs will be of great interest to you as well as everybody else. This evening, you're out and about with the newer faces in your circle, because they seem to have a great deal to say for themselves, which will prove to be illuminating, personally as well as on a professional level.

FEBRUARY

SATURDAY 1st Today looks as if the stars are giving you the chance to realize some of your dreams. The question is, are you alert enough to pick up on this? I certainly hope so, because you must be quick to grab opportunity when faced with it. Sometimes it seems that the more you try, the less you achieve, so the thing to do is to concentrate on what you see as your most inventive idea and use it well; others will be easily impressed.

SUNDAY 2nd You may be foolish enough to believe that family or other loved ones are ready to pander to your whims and ideas as well as fall in with all the changes you have in mind; if you're really convinced of this, you must be living on planet Zog. Change your tune and tactics and be ready to wait before making any further plans. Patience isn't, of course, your strong suit, but if you could develop just a little then you would find it much easier to realize your ambitions.

MONDAY 3rd Today, Venus moves into the air sign of Aquarius, joining three other planets, so clearly there's a great deal of attention and focus on friendships and acquaintances at this time. This is a good day for those of you who work in a team; some good news is likely to set your spirits rising. If you're fancy-free, an old friend may make an interesting introduction which could lead to a serious romance. Socialize this evening!

TUESDAY 4th It looks as if a new phase will soon be

starting in your working life and you can almost see it peeking over the horizon, but in the meanwhile this is an ideal day for treating yourself to a small present. There is nothing wrong with this as long as you don't go completely over the top. Alternatively, you could be extremely successful if you are considering buying or selling property. This evening will be perfect for home entertaining because you're just in the mood to act the role of host or hostess.

WEDNESDAY 5th   Uranus and Pluto are in a beautiful aspect today, so when it comes to your work contacts, you can expect one or two surprises and even shocks. Somebody is acting completely out of character, or possibly their ideas are so out of this world even you find them difficult to grasp, so they must be completely unrealistic. Nevertheless, it's an enjoyable time and if you're out with friends this evening you'll be letting off a steam in a big way.

THURSDAY 6th   Your ruling planet, Mars, now goes into retrograde movement, which means that from our position in space it seems to be going backward. From now on, you could begin to feel that for every pace you take forward, it's necessary to take three backwards and this will try your Arian patience quite severely. However, now you know this trend is about to descend, possibly you can adapt to the situation and in that way won't finish up a nervous wreck.

FRIDAY 7th   Today is New Moon day, which occurs in the sign of Aquarius where most of the other planets seem to be lurking. This suggests a minor new cycle beginning in the life of one of your closest friends. It also suggests that you'll be meeting new people, or perhaps the right word is 'cultivating', because you believe they can be useful to you. You'll need to be clever because it's hard for an Arian to indulge in any kind of dubious behaviour because you are invariably found out.

SATURDAY 8th Mercury is in a beautiful aspect with Neptune and so you need to keep on the go, for preference close to home as much as possible, particularly if you're looking for romance because brief encounters could come in multiples. You've plenty of creative ideas and should jot them down, because your head is already overcrowded with plans for the future and, if you're not careful, a real gem could slip your mind and you'll be kicking yourself for quite some time to come.

SUNDAY 9th Mercury moves into the sign of Aquarius and, because of this, you'll be attractive to the members of your circle who are reasonably intellectual; you want to do something more than just stand around drinking, you want intelligent conversation and need to go wherever you can find it. Romantically, someone could make an intro-duction to someone who sends the fire forcing through your veins.

MONDAY 10th Because the Moon is in your sign today, it definitely looks as if you're going to be in the thick of the action, but with your energy, you're unlikely to mind at all; what you do need is sufficient resourcefulness and endurance to survive. Although you may end the day feeling shattered, you will at least know that you have achieved a great deal and, because of this, may decide to treat yourself in some way.

TUESDAY 11th Your ruling planet, Mars, is lining up with Uranus and so there's a lively feel about the day and you too. You're a real 'live wire' with a head bursting full of incredible and fantastic ideas which you can't wait to explain to other people. Mind you, unless they jump up and down with enthusiasm, you'll feel a little disappointed though I think this an unlikely happening. After all, few of us can remain unmoved once that enterprising and enthusiastic side of your character comes to the surface.

WEDNESDAY 12th   Today, Mercury lines up in a beautiful aspect with Jupiter, so it's definitely a time for exercising the old grey matter. In fact, if you decide to enrol on any kind of course, you'll be doing yourself a big favour. Short-distance and long-distance travelling are well starred and you may even find romance whilst you're out and about; certainly this looks to be a day packed with action and one when you must be ready to recognize an opportunity when it hits you in the face.

THURSDAY 13th   Mercury is in a wonderful aspect with Uranus and so there seems to be a great deal of news and excitement in the friendship area of your life. Possibly one of your contacts is up to his or her neck in hot water and shouts for you, Mr or Ms Aries, because you're so good at charging in and helping other people. Naturally, you'll be building up a lot of goodwill for the future.

FRIDAY 14th   Your ruling planet, Mars, lines up with Pluto and this is quite an explosive aspect. You need to stay away from people who irritate or aggravate, because if you spend too much time with them, you could say far more than you meant to and then apologies will be necessary at a later date. Go where you know you can truly relax; be yourself and above all else, let off quite a lot of steam, because you've energy to burn.

SATURDAY 15th   It really is time, Aries, to sweep aside any guilty feelings you may have over something that happened a long while ago. This is vital if you are to make any kind of future progress. Nor should you be made to feel that you must explain recent moves to other people; this you resent anyway because, let's face it, you're a fire sign, which means you can grow into a roaring furnace or shrink to a pathetic spark unless your ego is fed quite regularly. And, if others aren't prepared to do this for you, you must do it for yourself.

SUNDAY 16th   Your ruling planet, Mars, is in a difficult aspect with Saturn today and so you may be picking up the odd cold-germ or perhaps tripping over your own feet. Whichever, it's certainly a day to watch your step, because a slight accident proneness could mean that you may miss out on something exciting this evening, which you will resent with great passion. A little caution takes you a long, long way.

MONDAY 17th   Friendship will almost certainly play an important part in your life today. Clearly then, it's a case of who you know and not what you know that's going to be of the utmost importance. Should anyone need you to give them some help, you'll gladly offer it, not because you're looking for any kind of thanks, but because you're a warm-hearted person who, although sometimes misguided, would never deliberately go out of your way to hurt another human being. You always do your best to be of help whenever you can. Now you've a chance to prove it.

TUESDAY 18th   There's a strong possibility that you want to change your lifestyle in some way, perhaps a partnership or an emotional problem has recently forced you to become more selective and independent. It certainly looks as if you are about to experience a re-awakening and, because you love a challenge, this won't phase you one little bit; you'll greet it with open arms in your usual enthusiastic way.

WEDNESDAY 19th   Today, the Sun will be moving into the watery sign of Pisces and so you begin a couple of weeks when you'll be quite happy to stay in the background of things for a change. Perhaps this is because you need to rethink a situation or lay down some plans for the future and are anxious not to be pushed or rushed, in case you make a wrong move. How very wise and how very unlike your sign. Make sure you use your instincts and intuition and you'll make the right judgement and can push ahead with your head held high.

THURSDAY 20th   It looks as if a special friend, contact or acquaintance may spring a surprise which is likely to lead eventually to an exciting change. At work, there's a feeling of exhilaration and optimism; perhaps a big deal is about to be signed or else something will happen which will make you realize that your situation is about to improve in a big way. This evening you could very well have reason for celebration, and won't shrink from doing so.

FRIDAY 21st   The Moon, in the fiery sign of Leo, puts you in something of a dramatic mood, so you may make very heavy weather of simple straightforward situations. Why don't you just use a little common sense and then a crisis can so easily be avoided? It may seem to you that things are rather inconclusive right now, but a little bit of patience will help you to work out what needs to be done and when. This evening is a good time for romance, though not if you're looking for the love of your life.

SATURDAY 22nd   Today is the Full Moon and it occurs in the earthy sign of Virgo. If you're working, you can certainly expect a complicated day and you'll be exhausted by the time you get home. If not, even a simple task around the home will sap your energy and, unless you pace yourself, you may have to cancel a social or emotional arrangement that you were looking forward to this evening. Full Moons must always be treated with a good deal of respect.

SUNDAY 23rd There are times, Aries, when you break the rules and rebel in no uncertain fashion and, when this occurs, nobody can stop you. Right now, you're finding it difficult to come to terms with developments in your personal life; you really must avoid bottling up your emotions, you know how unhealthy this is, so, if you feel like erupting, feel free to do so, because you can always apologize at a later date, if necessary.

MONDAY 24th The Sun is in a difficult aspect with Pluto and so if you're creative you could very well suffer from what is known as 'artist's block'. There's no point in fretting about this, that grey matter will soon unscramble itself once this day is through; in the meantime, turn your attention to little jobs, either at home or at work, that have been left undone and which don't demand a great deal of effort on your part. This evening it might be a good idea to spend time with somebody who can make you laugh.

TUESDAY 25th You'll be doing plenty of positive work in the background today and, if you're involved in any intense activity, it's certain that your progress will be remarkably swift, almost to the point where it may take your breath away. You may sense a feeling of tension between people you're visiting today and, because of this, will make sure that you don't overstay your welcome – how very wise!

WEDNESDAY 26th The stars suggest that domestic and property matters are going to be hectic and perhaps importantly decisive too. If you're typical of your Sign, you will thrive on any kind of opposition and verbal disagreement, you enjoy a good fight, particularly when you know you're in the right, as you seem to be this time. Even so, Aries, there's no need to crow, it won't make you popular.

THURSDAY 27th Today, Venus moves into the sign of

Pisces, and you begin a couple of weeks when you need to exercise a certain amount of caution where your emotional life is concerned, mainly because other people are being anything but open and honest with you. It may seem to you that they are fancy-free, but all the while they could have somebody tucked away in the background; you're an open person yourself and, it has to be said, are not above getting involved in complicated situations, but at least you like to be in the know.

FRIDAY 28th   It's unlike you to hang around for anyone or anything but, despite this, you appear to be waiting for other people to make the first move. It seems a good idea because the time is certainly not right to force the pace. You need to understand that other people are struggling with their consciences and complex emotions which, of course, is something you rarely suffer from. I'm not suggesting you don't have a conscience, but you are certainly less complicated than most other Signs.

MARCH

SATURDAY 1st   Although your resolve is strengthened by the fact that the Moon is in the fiery sign of Sagittarius, so is your tendency to dislike routine and, as a result, you will want to be changing much of what happens during the day. If you find yourself stuck indoors throughout this period, concentration will prove to be very difficult. Not only that, but your boredom could have some bizarre consequences which may surprise and even shock other people.

SUNDAY 2nd   Saturn is lining up with Uranus and this is sure to lead to better conditions in the very near future. Certainly it looks as if you'll be spending time with either an older friend or somebody who is in a very serious frame of mind, perhaps in desperate need of some advice. Naturally, as is generally the case, people listen and then do exactly what they wanted to do in the first place, but it's nice to be asked, to be thought of as a 'sounding board', because, at least, it shows someone cares for your opinion even if he or she may not act upon it.

MONDAY 3rd Mercury is in a beautiful aspect with Venus and, because of this, wherever you go, you're going to be greeted with lively faces and positively bombarded with good ideas, some of which you will take on; others are more likely to be jettisoned. Make sure you're out this evening because new people you meet may not only help you on the professional front, but also could prove to be extremely attractive, which you wouldn't want to miss.

TUESDAY 4th This is certainly an ideal time for thinking about travel plans, either for now or the future; you may also be casting your mind back to the past in order to glean some ideas. It's most important that you are not afraid to experiment in all areas of life at this time; being the crusader of the zodiac, this is most unlikely to occur, not if you're a typical Ram.

WEDNESDAY 5th Today, the stars may be tempting you into minor extravagances and, unless you can afford them, you really must fight and control such a mood. Ideally, the day should be spent working out professional or personal budgets, or meeting people who can help you with your finances, which are no doubt in a bit of a mess, which is probably par for the course for you!

THURSDAY 6th Regardless of your own sex, you are likely to discover your mother, and females in general, are more generous and helpful than males. But don't accept help unless it's absolutely necessary, because there will be most certainly a price to be paid in the near future.

Unfortunately, people rarely do anything for nothing, which you have to admit includes you.

FRIDAY 7th   Today, your ruling planet, Mars, moves into the earthy sign of Virgo due to its retrograde movement, so this means you could temporarily take on some of the characteristics associated with this Sign, becoming more picky and critical, but also more practical and down-to-earth. I'm not sure the change in you will be greatly appreciated by your loved ones, but they'll certainly be intrigued.

SATURDAY 8th   Pluto decides to go into retrograde movement which means that from our position in space it seems to be going backwards. While this state of affairs exists, which happens to be for quite some time, you must be more straightforward with officials and bureaucrats, because any attempt to hoodwink them will only backfire on you at a much later date. Try not to worry too much about the financial affairs of someone close to you, after all, no matter what advice you may give, they'll go and do exactly what they want to in the end.

SUNDAY 9th   Today is the New Moon and it occurs in the watery sign of Pisces which certainly will be heightening your sensitivity, your intuition and your imagination. This softer approach to life is sure to prove to be very popular with the opposite sex, so although there may be a tendency for you to want to 'hole up' this evening, it might be better for you to make the effort and get out into the big wide world, because I doubt that you'll regret it. A new romance is only one of the possibilities waiting for you.

MONDAY 10th   It looks as if you have finally realized that someone special means the whole world to you, even though it's a strong possibility that you may be miles apart. You may think they underestimate you, but don't be misled, their feelings for you are just as strong as they ever were and will at some point change your life, perhaps for ever.

TUESDAY 11th   Mercury is in a beautiful aspect with the Sun, today, and so you'll be whizzing through paperwork, which has been allowed to pile up, in record time. This is a great day for signing on the dotted line, and will eventually lead to greater wealth. And, this evening, you'll be the life and soul of any gathering you attend, so make sure you're not found skulking around at home feeling sorry for yourself; just make that extra effort because you'll be glad that you did.

WEDNESDAY 12th   You know, Aries, you really ought to think about holding back and examining your conscience where a relationship is concerned, not so much because of what it meant in the past, but because, in the light of present circumstances, you may see things very differently. If you're out and about this evening, there'll be a strong tendency for you to give in to extravagant impulses, so unless you have your own 'Fort Knox' tucked away somewhere, it'll be a good idea to put on your 'sensible head'.

THURSDAY 13th   You're in an excellent position today to overcome any disagreements between yourself and those who influence your life. Creative aspects will help to encourage exciting ideas, but be wary of becoming too romantic; you are apt to get carried away and then feel hurt when you're misunderstood. If you're not careful, you may have some explaining to do later on in the week.

FRIDAY 14th   Perhaps you have entered the fray once too often, because there's a lot to deal with in your life at this time. The usual way of applying yourself unstintingly to a job is perhaps impossible right now, when circumstances keep changing. Fortunately, the stars bring a tempting new diversion your way. A change of scene promises refreshment to your very soul.

SATURDAY 15th New choices presented to you, today, could seem to be much sought-after balm for your current discomforture. At least your sense of security has never been affected by ghosts from the past. As an Aries, you are too open-minded ever to become imprisoned by disappointment and, no matter how unreliable friends or workmates may have been, what always interests you is what you can make of the future.

SUNDAY 16th Mercury moves into your sign and this will certainly be livening you up both physically and mentally. In the next few weeks or so, good ideas will be popping into your brain, even when you're half-asleep. It might be a good idea to keep pen and paper handy, because you're quite likely to forget them in the clear light of day, which would be a shame. Those of you who are travelling over the next couple of weeks, can be sure that you will enjoy yourself, as well as make a profit for your company or firm, if you're doing so on a professional basis.

MONDAY 17th Spoiling yourself should be on the top of your list of priorities today, instead of running around after other people. Any interest or activity that boosts your morale and sense of well-being will help to dismiss the feeling that however much you give to someone else, there is still an underlying expectation that you could do more. What makes you attractive to others, in the first place, is your sense of fun. Don't allow anyone to put out your fire.

TUESDAY 18th Mercury is lining up with Pluto and this could result in several changes of mind, on and off throughout the day. Don't leap into any kind of action, until you have finally settled upon the right solution or direction, otherwise it may be necessary for you to rethink and start all over again. With your small degree of patience, no one in their right mind would expect you to keep your sanity under such conditions.

WEDNESDAY 19th   There's always a time to come up for air, Aries, and explore the surface rather than the depths, and for you that time could be now. You could do with releasing your possessive grip on certain challenges, because they seem to be consuming you and burning a new desire for finding a middle way in life. It's important that you make time for yourself for a change. Remember that the clever fish doesn't always rise to the bait.

THURSDAY 20th   Mercury is in a beautiful aspect with Neptune today and, because of this, you're all fired up with creative and original ideas, hopefully you manage to find a channel for them otherwise you could become frustrated. Luckily, you're romantic and so if you've someone special in your life, he or she is certainly in for a great deal of attention during this evening; if not, get out with friends because you never know what could happen.

FRIDAY 21st   Today the Sun moves into your Sign and so you begin your own personal zodiac year. A time for pushing ahead with everything of interest to you, with that wonderful flair and enthusiasm which invariably manages to impress everybody you meet. As a rule, most astrologers tend to discourage the 'me first' side of your character, but during the next few weeks, this is a time which is yours and yours alone.

SATURDAY 22nd   This day is sure to be an important one for you when it comes to making agreements. This is because there is so much astrological action in your own particular Sign. So, however much you feel like rushing headlong towards opportunities, firstly, examine thoroughly the small print in business or the bottom line in personal relationships. Because, right now, recklessness could cost you dear in the month ahead.

SUNDAY 23rd Venus moves into your Sign and, over the next couple of weeks, you will blossom before our very eyes. Physically, you'll be irresistible and, mentally, at your most charming, so this is most definitely a time for chasing what and whom you want, because others find you difficult to resist, so why not take advantage of this?

MONDAY 24th The Full Moon, today, occurs in your opposite sign of Libra, so you may find those closest to you a little tetchy, insecure or bad tempered. Instead of throwing one of your furious tantrums, try to discover exactly what is wrong and then talk things through sensibly, because communication is the only way that any relationship can survive. Without it you might just as well stay on your own.

TUESDAY 25th Your capacity to enjoy yourself is growing with pleasure-loving Venus moving into your Sign. Although this magnetic planet can't wave a magic wand over your life or your relationships, it will cast a warm glow around you that melts even the frostiest heart. Even if you have to cross swords over money, you are likely to emerge feeling the result was well worth the effort.

WEDNESDAY 26th Someone close to you may try to force your hand, but to give up your right of control now would be to sacrifice all that is sacred to you. You need to find a logical solution that will not harm the situation. Only time will reveal whether you really are on the right track personally or professionally. For now, all you can do is to have the courage of your convictions and be strong.

THURSDAY 27th   Venus is in a beautiful aspect with
Pluto, today, which is all very well, but it's going to make
those closest to you extremely turbulent and changeable.
Mind you, they're likely to be very physical and this, of
course, you won't object to at all. The thing to remember
is to adapt to their mood and not to insist on having your
own way; by taking this tack, you will be building a lot
of goodwill and love for the future.

FRIDAY 28th   The Sun is beautifully aspected by Uranus
and so there's a 'fun' feel about the day. You seem to be
in demand, both socially and emotionally, and may have
a hard time making up your mind exactly who you want
to spend your time with – what a lovely position to find
yourself in! Certainly friends will be in touch more than
is usually the case and it looks as if your diary is going
to be fully booked over the next couple of weeks or so.

SATURDAY 29th   This is a time when you need to hold
the things that you want, or wish for, in your imagination,
if they are to become a reality. Right now, you are really
tuned into the stars and, because of this, only the correct
mixture of faith, hope and will-power will achieve what
you want out of life. Aries, you can do it, you really can!

SUNDAY 30th   The Sun is in a beautiful aspect with
Saturn and, although you may have been muddled and
confused about exactly what your next professional move
should be, today it becomes all too obvious to you, and
you can't wait to get back to work tomorrow. Meanwhile,
give plenty of time to your loved ones, because it's likely
that recently they've been sadly neglected, while you have
been wrestling with which direction you should be going
in next. Now you know, there's no excuse for holding back
your Aries warmth.

MONDAY 31st   Today, Venus is in a lovely aspect with

Saturn and, because of this, those closest to you are full of wonderful ideas and good advice, if only you can be persuaded to shelve your independent side and listen to what they have to say. It's likely that you'll be taking a much more serious attitude towards one of your relationships and some of you may be preparing to make a commitment. It's a lovely way to end any month.

APRIL

TUESDAY 1st   This month begins with a sparkling aspect between Venus and the Sun so you're certainly full of the joys of living. Wherever you go, other people seem to be tripping over their feet in a rush to do you favours, ask you to join them socially, and flatter your ego to such a degree that you could be impossible to live with by the time the evening comes. Never mind, Aries, bask in all this popularity, but make sure you give back a little in return, because this is something you occasionally forget to do.

WEDNESDAY 2nd   Today, the Moon in Aquarius will certainly help to calm troubled waters. On the other hand, if a partner, be it professional or personal, is unwilling to be more open-minded and flexible, it may well be the time to find a more deserving companion. Right now a major upheaval may seem the only logical response to a problem, but very soon the groundwork will be done, and you will then be able to take your time to ring one or two changes.

THURSDAY 3rd   You're certainly going to be making an impact on the world at large, but you must pick the best area in which to concentrate all your efforts. The stars suggest that you're preparing for one of the most important periods of the year. What's more, as a very strong and determined fire sign, you don't always welcome the thought of moving around or even travelling unless you deem it to be necessary. However, you can rest assured because with so much on your side, you can't put a foot wrong, unless, of course, you really try.

FRIDAY 4th   Venus is in a wonderful aspect with Jupiter today and so it won't pay you to be your usual dynamic and independent self. Like it or not, Aries, we all need other people at some time and this is most certainly a time for remembering this; others are lucky and imaginative and will be able to give you a fresh slant on old problems, as well as contributing a great deal to your social life this evening. If you've had your eye on a member of the opposite sex for some time now, this is a great evening for making a move.

SATURDAY 5th   We really do seem to be spoiled for good aspects this month, so far anyway. Today, the Sun is in a wonderful aspect with Jupiter, making it a lucky time for dealing with matters related to education or affairs abroad. Sports, children and romance all have a happy glow about them, and so if there's something you want to change or talk through in these areas, put aside excuses and jump in head first, as you usually do. Just for a change, you'll be saying the right thing at the right time.

SUNDAY 6th   Today, Mercury lines up with Pluto, so it is certainly not a day for asserting yourself where officials and bureaucrats are concerned because, if you do, you're likely to get your wrists slapped. Stick to the letter of the law, and catch up on routine work which has, no doubt, been neglected, even if it's only around the house. Also, try to find a way to truly relax this evening; remember it's the company you keep which will please, rather than any particular activity.

MONDAY 7th   Today is the day of the New Moon and

it falls in your Sign. How can you go wrong? Only with a great deal of difficulty and determination. You are slap-bang in the middle of the limelight and lapping up all the attention, which no doubt is deserved. If you want to present changes to your family, your boss or to that special person in your life, you couldn't have a better time because they'll be able to see your point of view and will agree with you 100 per cent. Aries, you can certainly get your own way on this particular day. Don't let it go to waste.

TUESDAY 8th The stars today are in cracking form and seem to suggest you can look forward to favourable changes within the family or at home, which will have a positive effect on your life as well as your work. It seems that an unconventional approach may be the only way to resolve a long-standing problem, so say what you mean, mean what you say and things will definitely improve. In love, you seem to be involved in a little bit of plotting and scheming, which is most unusual for you and so you need to take care because you could be found out.

WEDNESDAY 9th Mercury is in a difficult aspect with Uranus today and, because of this, concentration could be elusive. You can't seem to make up your mind about anything at this time which is very unusual, but don't fret about this; after all you are only human, despite other people's belief to the contrary. The best thing to do is to avoid anything which needs a great deal of attention and try to devise a way for letting off steam this evening, because I think you're going to need it.

THURSDAY 10th Today the stars suggest that the better you feel within yourself, in your relationship, the more progress you'll make in other areas, so it's very much a case of putting your personal life first, for a change. Naturally, you are fiercely ambitious, being a typical Ram, but there are times when other considerations need your attention and this is one of them. Try to arrange something special for the person who is most important to you and this will provide you with a chance to relax, which is much needed right now.

FRIDAY 11th   You, of course, like to be at the top, but unless you control your cash flow, rivals may undermine you. In the past, restrictions seem to have thwarted your progress in all directions but life needn't be like that today. Harness the energies the stars are providing, push forward and remember you are an asset in anything connected with your job or money.

SATURDAY 12th   The Moon in the airy sign of Gemini could very well clear up doubts or confirm suspicions, but you must keep a tight lid on arrangements and plans until acceptable solutions or answers are presented; then you'll start a new, more productive and positive phase all round. Romantically, don't take your emotions too seriously as they are easily moved; what looks like a promising proposition today could look like Godzilla tomorrow.

SUNDAY 13th   Today is an ideal time for putting your own house in order. If you don't, you'll set an uneasy tone for the next month or so. Try to avoid making arrangements which mean heavy financial commitment. If there are already plans in motion, be ready for certain set-backs. Involve others; meetings and talks with relatives will bring results and a heart to heart with a lover will help you to draw strength.

MONDAY 14th   Today, Mercury decides to go into retrograde movement, which means that from our position in space it seems to be going backwards. You'll need to take extra care with what you say, or write, whilst this state of affairs exists. Communications need to be double-checked and instructions you give made abundantly clear and straightforward. If anything is left to chance you can be quite sure it'll result in a gigantic muddle which will take time to unravel. So slow down a little, Aries, and all should be well.

TUESDAY 15th   Venus moves into Taurus today and you begin a period where finances certainly seem to be well starred. Certainly if we are around your birthday, you'll be doing extremely well where gifts are concerned. Those of you who work in the arts will be well rewarded for all your efforts, so much so that you will feel that you can afford to splash out on one or two luxuries; fine, as long as you don't go completely over-the-top, Aries; use some common sense.

WEDNESDAY 16th   Venus is in a difficult aspect with Neptune today and so you can't rely on other people for anything; they are confused, muddled and dreamy; so as long as you stay your usual independent self you'll be able to sidestep potential problems. This evening, on no account allow yourself to become emotionally carried away; you may be able to convince yourself that a sexual attraction means a great deal and this could lead to hurt in the future.

THURSDAY 17th   You're fairly confident today but please don't get carried away or believe that minimum effort will bring in big results, because it won't. There are several unlikely schemes in the air and you'd be better off concentrating on more worthwhile projects. Although what happens in the future isn't entirely reliant on what you do right now, you must respond correctly and open your eyes to certain home truths.

FRIDAY 18th   Because this continues to be your time of the year, in many ways, it's something of a 'crunch time', and the more open you are to disruption, the better. Not that it's all bad – the stars mark the end of one romantic relationship and the beginning of another. In the end, you'll accept there's no longer a place in your life for people who have been unable to grow in the same way as you have. Increased security is one likely outcome of current events.

SATURDAY 19th Do be careful today because the Sun is lining up with Neptune and you could be carried away on a fluffy pink cloud of romance. Yes, you're flying away in the outer stratosphere without so much as a little toe connected to the ground! You'll be able to fool yourself into believing literally anything and others will find you an easy target. Once you recognize this fact, you may be able to enjoy yourself, but failure to do so could find you sobbing your heart out at a later date.

SUNDAY 20th Mercury is in a difficult aspect with Uranus today and, because of this, you find it difficult to make up your mind about anything, most unusual for an Aries. One minute you think you want one person or object and the next something else. Those closest to you could be tearing their hair out with frustration and you won't have a clue as to why they're behaving in such an unreasonable fashion. Look in the mirror, Aries; think about what you're saying, and what you're about to do, and then you'll understand the reason for their concern.

MONDAY 21st Today the Sun moves into the earthy sign of Taurus, which is the cash area of your life and so you are provided with a few weeks when you are able to save and conserve rather than splurge. Luckily, your attitude will change and you will be reluctant to do anything for anybody for nothing; if somebody wants you to work overtime you will expect to be well rewarded, and justly so too. This is a good time for the collector who may be buying something really special. You'll shine at financial meetings too, because no one can pull the wool over your eyes at this time.

TUESDAY 22nd   Today is the day of the Full Moon and it occurs in the watery sign of Scorpio. This is a clear warning to make absolutely certain that you stick to the letter of the law when dealing with bureaucrats and officials, because any attempt at deviation could land you in hot water. Wherever possible avoid making important decisions or starting anything fresh. Instead, use this time for learning from the past and putting the finishing touches to work. Making plans would also be a good idea.

WEDNESDAY 23rd   The Moon in the water sign of Scorpio suggests that when it comes to any kind of financial relationship or financial matter, thought and decisive action are needed, and this is just the kind of advice you like. If one romantic relationship has come to an end, get ready to start a new one. If not, talks and discussions are the only hope for you to get this affair back to normal.

THURSDAY 24th   There's a happy feel about this particular day; a few understandings are being reached. And, if life or love has lost its lustre, the stars today will soon put it back. What's more, you'll be sensing a favourable change in the wind. Your luck is certainly in, but if there are risky plans you want to get off the launching pad, make sure you do so under favourable aspects.

FRIDAY 25th   The Sun is in a beautiful aspect with Mercury and so you can attend to travel matters, meetings, negotiations and paperwork with relative ease and far more patience than is usually the case. You won't want to stay in this evening, because you're physically restless and, as you travel around, old friends will be making interesting introductions which could lead to useful contacts, romance or simply just the chance to swell your circle of friends.

SATURDAY 26th   As a rule, you're very good at helping others but now it's your turn to be on the receiving end of other people's time and energy. If you start to assert yourself a little more, you'll be gaining greater respect for yourself, and will be opening up good opportunities too. It may be best to keep plans in reserve and play safe. The longer you hold your cards to your chest, the better your chances of hitting the jackpot at a later date. Workmates may scoff, but if you can stop fretting about what might happen or what they think, you'll get a lot further.

SUNDAY 27th   At last, your ruling planet, Mars, resumes direct movement, which means you lose that feeling of one step forward and half a dozen backwards. From now on, your progress in all areas of life should be much smoother and more successful. Physically, you'll begin to blossom, too, mainly because you're feeling so much more relaxed. Tension and stress are always the worst things for our looks, regardless of whether we're male or female; take a look in the mirror and you'll probably see somebody who looks at least five years younger. And all without even a touch of the surgeon's knife.

MONDAY 28th   The Sun is in a difficult aspect with Uranus today and, because of this, friends and contacts could be unreliable and their judgement completely awry. So, Aries, be your usual independent self, push out into life on your own, because it's likely you know exactly what needs to be done, when and how. Certainly, mix with your pals this evening, but don't take them too seriously; there are matters in the background of their lives which are leading them to behave in such an odd fashion.

TUESDAY 29th   A beautiful aspect between Venus and Mars certainly bodes well for co-operation and harmony in all of your relationships. If you're fancy-free you may meet someone really special or, if you're in a relationship which has been teetering on the edge of disaster, you may finally be able to rescue it before things go too far. Professional partnerships are also well starred, so the more you co-operate today the better your time will be spent.

WEDNESDAY 30th   Although the stars are preparing you for a new stage in your life, it's pointless counting your chickens, at least for another couple of weeks or so. By this time, you'll be able to see whether your ideas are successful or whether you need to get back to the drawing board and rethink. The important thing to do is be objective; the stars suggest that the more impartial you are, the greater your performance will be.

MAY

THURSDAY 1st   Very soon you'll find out how far you have come and just how much further you need to travel. You seem to be learning a great deal this year, but even so the position of Neptune at the zenith of your chart makes you impressionable and easily deceived, particularly where work matters are concerned, so you need to take care if you're in an ambitious mood. Put off all you can, and concentrate on people and places who are at a distance. It's not an ideal day for travelling, but it's a great one for planning and, with enough forethought, you can make the best of everything.

FRIDAY 2nd   The Moon, in the watery sign of Pisces, in many ways supplies some pinpricks to your confidence; on the one hand, you have tremendous energy and can't wait to start pushing ahead and getting your own way, but on the other hand, there are little doubts niggling away at the back of your mind. The best advice is for you to sit, reflect and try to work out exactly what you want out of life and, having done so, pick a really good day, during this particular month, for going for it. In the meantime, why not turn your attention to relaxation and perhaps the family; no doubt they are feeling neglected.

SATURDAY 3rd   Usually you're an upfront kind of person but now, for reasons best known to yourself, you seem to be involved in a certain amount of manipulation from behind the scenes, you're definitely playing the puppeteer; don't take this too far. Your imagination is working at full throttle and so you need to keep busy. Get on the telephone and make sure that every hour is filled with activity and, ideally, in the company of those who can really make you laugh. We all need a time for letting stresses and strains simply melt away and this is one for you.

SUNDAY 4th   Aries, you really must go out of your way today to be a little more giving and thoughtful. The people who are important in your life seem to be ready to start talking problems through; luckily, you are the sort of person who thrives on confrontation and so now you have a chance to explain your feelings and say exactly what has been bothering you over recent weeks. A word of warning though; for heaven's sake use a certain amount of tact and charm, because you can be a little too straightforward and honest on occasions!

MONDAY 5th   Mercury is in a difficult aspect with Neptune today and so you'll have the unhappy knack of being able to fool yourself into believing anything you want to. Yes, self-deception is rife and so it would be a good idea to listen to what you find yourself saying, and where it is at fault; don't be too proud to retract.

This is clearly not a time for making important moves, whether they be domestic or emotional. Why not use this particular evening for resting up and leave the world to its own devices for the time being.

TUESDAY 6th This is the day of the New Moon and, luckily for you, it occurs in the cash area of life, so there could be some good financial news waiting for you and, in some instances, perhaps even a fresh source of income. A late birthday present is another possibility, and it's certainly a good time for financial meetings, because you'll positively shine with confidence. As always with New Moons, it's important to keep in the limelight because as an Aries, you'd hate to miss out.

WEDNESDAY 7th Lucky you, there seems to be plenty of attractive opportunities and propositions heading in your direction. Even so, you won't be able to take advantage of them, for the time being, because you need to balance them against the responsibilities you have to your loved ones. Control that Aries impulse to rush in, and think things through at a later date – because often it is too late and today could be a classic example.

THURSDAY 8th Your money planet, Mercury, has finally decided to see sense and resume direct movement, so cash matters should run a great deal more smoothly over the next few weeks or so. You can now sign contracts and attend interviews and meetings with that extra little bit of confidence in the sure knowledge that you will succeed as long as you don't go over-the-top. Those who travel for professional reasons are in for a profitable as well as a happy time. If youngsters have been playing up, at home, now is an ideal time for sitting them down and finding out what their problem really is.

FRIDAY 9th This can be an exceptionally lucky day if

you work or play as a member of a team, or, if you are
a freelance worker trying to make a sincere effort to get
people interested in your talents, you'll quickly find that
they are more approachable than they have been for some
time and so your day, in the main, should be a success.
This evening, invitations which come in from old friends
or acquaintances should be snapped up without further
ado, because not only would they provide you with a
couple of hours of fun and games, but also in some way
or other they could be useful too.

SATURDAY 10th Because you're basically a child at
heart, Aries, you can invariably identify with people who
are a good deal younger or perhaps less experienced than
yourself, because you remember what it felt like to be
not only a teenager but also perhaps a child. This will
certainly help you to heal rifts that your own generation
finds impossible to understand and you will most certainly
be getting a great deal in the way of appreciation and
thanks from youngsters. This evening, don't spend money
in order to impress the opposite sex; all you have to be is
your usual fiery and dynamic self.

SUNDAY 11th The Sun today is in a difficult aspect
with Uranus, so don't be surprised if your social, or even
your romantic, arrangements come in for some last-minute
changes. You may find that somebody else's unreliability
jars on your nerves, but you'd be wise to keep your very
fiery mouth shut for the time being; you can talk through
differences, perhaps, at a better time, at a later date.

MONDAY 12th Today, Venus moves into the airy sign
of Gemini which will certainly help to improve your
self-expression; you'll be using charm rather than force,
persuasion rather than threats and this planet's effect on
your love life is likely to be significant. For the next couple
of weeks, there'll be many brief encounters so you need to

keep your eyes wide open, otherwise you could seriously miss out.

TUESDAY 13th   Today, Uranus decides to go into retrograde movement, which means from our position in space it seems to be going backwards. Because of this, friends and contacts may let you down when you most need them, but you must not allow your temper to erupt like a volcano; try to put yourself in their position, because in this way you may be able to understand. Perhaps they had no intention of letting you down, but circumstances made it difficult for them to keep formal promises they had made to you. Aries, that's life; these things sometimes happen, so try to be as philosophical as you can be.

WEDNESDAY 14th   Today, Venus is in a difficult aspect with Pluto and, unless you're careful, there could be serious damage to your bank account. Avoid unnecessary expenses as well as glitzy shops because you'll be so easily tempted. Remember, too, that you don't have to spend in order to impress the opposite sex, and also that the amount of money you splash out won't necessarily bring you enjoyment. Instead, opt for the company of people who really understand you and who share a similar sense of humour; that's the way to get the most out of your evening.

THURSDAY 15th   Today seems to be a highly ambitious time for one reason or another. The only trouble is that when Rams focus everything on ambition and worldly success, they do tend to neglect most other areas of life. If you do so at the moment, you can expect to hear some very loud complaints from those who mean a great deal to you. The answer is to try to create some kind of balance; it's not easy, Aries, but you like a challenge!

FRIDAY 16th   Today, the stars suggest that lately you

have been working extremely hard, not only for yourself but for the benefit of other people, particularly loved ones. This becomes clear when you're flooded with sentimental feelings and new resolve. Your opposite sign is Libra and, because of this, you are supposed to learn something. Libra is associated with balance, therefore Aries, if you can do a little clever juggling, you'll be able to keep everybody happy, including yourself; it is up to you to try.

SATURDAY 17th   You seem to be in a happy-go-lucky mood today, passing on cheerful news to other people and receiving a promise, as well as plenty of compliments, from the opposite sex. Naturally, some of you will be at work and, if so, things won't be as pleasant as they have been, and there may be a clash between a career interest and your leisure-time. You've a tough decision to make here; you must always bear in mind that you can't please everybody all the time and, if you attempt to do so, you're just going to run yourself ragged, which will never do.

SUNDAY 18th   Venus is in a beautiful aspect with Uranus today and so there's a strong possibility of an unforgettable attraction. Somebody may make your impulsive heart beat like thunder, but before you rush in where angels fear to tread, it might be a good idea to put out a few feelers and make sure that he or she is, at least, interested in you, because your ego simply can't stand rejection. If you already have a partner, be prepared to go along with their plans, because they're more original than your own.

MONDAY 19th   Now that the Moon has moved into your opposite sign of Libra, the emphasis is definitely going to be on the intensely personal side of life and everybody who means a great deal to you. Others seem to be bursting with good ideas; the only question is, are you going to give them enough time to explain them to you? This evening, you certainly won't be found lacking if you find that somebody has got him or herself into a spot of 'hot water'; you'll charge in like the proverbial knight in armour with as much help as you can muster. For other Rams, casual contact with those who live close by could very well lead to romance, so there's no point in travelling too far away, as everything seems to be on your own doorstep.

TUESDAY 20th The Sun is in a beautiful aspect with Neptune today, so there's a sentimental but inspirational feel about the day. Certainly if your work is at all artistic, your ideas will be astounding other people and you'll be making a great impression. If, on the other hand, you're wondering whether or not to push ahead where a romance is concerned, let me tell you, you're receiving the green light from the stars, so off you go! However, it might be a good idea to hold a little back in reserve, just in case the object of your affections is harbouring one or two little doubts. After all, some of us become distinctly uncomfortable when we are swept off our feet by a Ram, because we wonder just how long the enthusiasm is going to last; it's not known for its longevity.

WEDNESDAY 21st You couldn't have a better time for making plans for the long-term future, but on no account should you put them into action for the time being; so control your impulsive head. Cashwise, there'll be chances to make a new beginning, perhaps even a change of direction, but you won't be able to do it without a certain amount of difficulty; luckily, you are one Sign who enjoys a challenge so you're unlikely to be thrown off balance simply because something doesn't immediately fall into your lap. This evening you seem to be getting into heated debates with acquaintances. Make sure these don't deteriorate into fierce arguments; you know how hot-tempered you can be.

THURSDAY 22nd Today is the day of the Full Moon

and it occurs in the fiery sign of Sagittarius. So, if you are hoping to hear from somebody from abroad, for one reason or another, the call could be delayed. In general it's not a time to turn your attention to travel matters, because if you book a holiday now you may live to regret it in the future. Those of you who are studying may find that information is difficult to assimilate and you could become impatient. Bear in mind that this is Full Moon day so don't expect things to run smoothly. Use your day for making plans; don't make important moves because you'll be beaten before you even get started.

FRIDAY 23rd   Today, the Sun moves into the airy sign of Gemini, so over the next few weeks the emphasis will be shifting onto the affairs of brothers and sisters and communications of all descriptions. If you work by sales or advertising, your confidence will be growing in leaps and bounds. Romantically, there'll be many chances of meeting new people, but they file past before your very eyes without lingering for any length of time. Yes, you're at your most flirtatious, so if you have a partner, you'd better watch out because the green-eyed goddess of jealousy will be rearing her ugly head.

SATURDAY 24th   Mercury is in a difficult aspect with Uranus, today, and unfortunately this could very well mean that you'll say the wrong thing, at the wrong time, to the wrong person. If you are looking for a showdown with somebody, it will be a good idea to do your homework before you let rip, otherwise you'll make a fool of yourself. You know how proud you can be, and then your only defence is arrogance, which won't exactly boost you in the popularity poll! A little caution today will help you out no end.

SUNDAY 25th   The Sun is in a difficult aspect with Pluto so on no account should you take liberties with the law in any way; you won't get away with it. You may be worrying about somebody else's ability to carry on contributing to the family budget, maybe they've hit a bad patch, but don't jump to conclusions, instead, sit them down and have a sensible conversation so that you can discover exactly what their plans for the future are. Far better to do this than to erupt like a volcano, because then apologies will be needed at a later date and with your fierce pride, this isn't an easy thing for you to do.

MONDAY 26th   Today you become very practical and even money-grubbing. For one reason or another you've suddenly become anxious to save your hard-earned cash and won't do anything for nothing, no matter how good the cause may seem. Yes, you definitely expect to be well rewarded for all your efforts and there's no reason why you shouldn't be. Heaven help anyone who tries to take advantage of you at this time, because you are certainly not lacking in confidence.

TUESDAY 27th   That woolly coat of yours will become all tangled up with aggravation because you seem to be caught on the horns of some kind of dilemma. Calm down, my Ram-like friend, and see what you can do to use your intuition, because it is far better to respond to your feelings right now, than to what you think to be right. Clinical analysis of any situation will, for a change, lead you completely astray. What you need to do is to react instinctively to what is going on around you and then you'll discover that you really can't go wrong; you should be able to calm down and take life at a more serene pace.

WEDNESDAY 28th   Venus is in a beautiful aspect with Jupiter and so it's difficult to imagine you getting through the day without somehow becoming just that little bit richer, either in experience or where the bank account is concerned. Don't be too independent because other people are lucky for you and will be passing on some wise advice, which should be taken seriously. You may even discover that somebody you've known for quite some while has developed a real crush on you; very flattering and also very promising.

THURSDAY 29th   The Sun is in a beautiful aspect with Uranus and so there's a lively, unexpected, sparkling feel about this particular day which should be providing even you with enough activity to keep you happy. Invitations to fun or romance which come completely from a surprise direction should be snapped up immediately, because it is the unusual which will be appealing to you at this time. Mind you, if it's necessary for you to cancel a long-made arrangement, do so with a certain amount of charm because you really can't afford to lose an old friend; none of us can.

FRIDAY 30th   Recently, some of you may have been feeling rather unenthusiastic, listless, even pessimistic and if so, today you should reach a turning point and once more be ready to take on the world and everybody in it. Heaven help the rest of us once you get cracking, because there's no stopping the Ram when it's in full charge. Now is the time to tackle those tricky business deals and those awkward customers, because you are in a position to talk your way around any potentially difficult situation; even if it resembles a minefield, you will survive.

SATURDAY 31st   Cash matters seem to be well starred today, which either means you're getting good value for money, or if you're really lucky, some of you may experience a win or discover you have more of this lovely stuff tucked away in the bank than you had expected. Mind you, be warned that this is no excuse for mad extravagances; Lady Luck could desert you just as suddenly as she appeared; always remember that. When it comes to dealing with newly made friends or acquaintances, use your instincts instead of your intellect, because they'll be steering you in the right direction. Very much a case of heart over mind today!

JUNE

SUNDAY 1st Luckily, the stars in the firmament are having a positive influence on you. You're feeling much more optimistic about the future and, because that Aries positive thinking is on the rampage, you are sure to attract some good luck, in one way or another. A romantic encounter which has been dormant may suddenly spring into life and take you by surprise, but if you already have a partner, you'll need to do some fast talking.

MONDAY 2nd If you're a salesperson, or simply an individual who wants to offload a possession that has been hanging around for simply ages, you'll find that your persuasive powers are building up, giving you greater confidence and so this shouldn't present you with any kind of difficulty. Certainly, in all areas, you appear to be at your most persuasive, so now could also be the time for a quiet word with people of influence, because, in one way or another, they may be able to advance your wishes, hopes and dreams. Make sure that you get out this evening because there's fun and love in the air; it may be a Monday, but that doesn't mean Cupid goes to sleep!

TUESDAY 3rd A matter that has been troubling your mind for quite some time seems to come to a head. The outcome of all this could be surprising, and force you into making a reluctant choice. It's a time to be a little suspicious; you must be wary of those who are going out of their way to be friendly, because either they have ulterior motives, or it's simply a case of them being so fickle that they will be giving you a run for your money and, quite frankly, you don't need the aggravation at the moment.

WEDNESDAY 4th   Today, Venus moves into the watery sign of Cancer and this will be easing any tensions which may exist between you and your family or flatmate. It's going to be a good few weeks for pushing ahead with property matters and, if you want to do any special entertaining, you're positively going to shine; so I suspect there could be a good deal of mixing business with pleasure for various reasons. And why not? At least you're pretty open about your desires and others find this difficult to resist.

THURSDAY 5th   Today is the day of the New Moon and it falls in the mischievous sign of Gemini. This speeds up your already active head, and so it will be a good idea to slow yourself down a little in order to avoid making mistakes. Certainly you'll want to keep on the go from morning till night and, in the process, will be making new contacts; you may find yourself totally swept off your feet by an interesting stranger, although you may not have a chance to develop the relationship for the time being.

FRIDAY 6th   Mercury, in touch with Mars today, makes you far more adaptable and ready to listen to the ideas and suggestions of other people. When you do, you may be gleaning an answer to a long-standing problem, so my advice to you is to be a little less self-reliant, be open-minded to what other people are saying, because they certainly could be lucky for you at this time. This is also a good day for signing on the dotted line.

SATURDAY 7th   Mercury lines up with Pluto and, where normally you know exactly what you want out of life and what you don't, today you seem to be in a lather of indecision; don't knock this, it's simply a case of the stars giving you sufficient time to think, and even rethink, before you make your next important move in some area of life. You may be receiving strange letters from an official source, but don't allow yourself to be intimidated, there may be a computer fault here. If so, get on the phone, stay polite, but point out the error of their ways.

SUNDAY 8th   Right now, you're at your most ambitious, unfortunately, being a Sunday, there is little you can do about this except perhaps make a few phone calls and lay down some plans for the future. It will pay you to stay in the centre of all the action, particularly if you're looking for romance, because it's not totally out of the question at this time. A much older person will be passing on some wise words, the question is are you going to listen?

MONDAY 9th   Today, Mercury moves into Gemini, which will certainly be gingering you up, both mentally and physically, and you'll need to be particularly careful if your work requires a great deal of concentration because it may be seriously lacking. Make sure that you're out and about this evening, burning off some excess enthusiasm which could make you highly strung. Over the next couple of weeks, you'll be making new contact with people who can influence your life in a very positive way.

TUESDAY 10th   Mercury's difficulty with Pluto, today, could mean that your thought processes could break down at any moment; in order to offset this, apply yourself to that which you know like the back of your hand and avoid taking on new challenges for the time being. If you're travelling any distance, this evening, it might be a good idea to allow plenty of time to get to your destination and take things slowly, as opposed to trying to break all land-speed records.

WEDNESDAY 11th   Venus is in aspect with Uranus today so the 'urge to splurge' could be upon you in a big way; when an Aries decides to be extravagant you don't do it by halves, but you usually live to regret it. Avert your eyes from the 'glitzy' shops and in that way you may be able to stay solvent, well, for a little while anyway. There's an unexpected feel about romance, and if you have a date lined up this evening, it might be a good idea to do a little double-checking, because there's nothing you hate more than being left hanging around.

THURSDAY 12th The Sun lines up with Uranus today bringing interesting, although eccentric, new people into your life. Certainly, if you work as a member of a team, there may be a sudden breakthrough which will delight you. This evening, visits to clubs are likely to be exciting and thrilling because in some way or other you could run across somebody who will be pulling at your heart strings. If you're in a steady relationship, make sure that you behave yourself, because you'll certainly live to regret it if you don't.

FRIDAY 13th That eccentric planet, Uranus, seems to be very busy these days; it is again lining up with a planet, only this time the heavenly body concerned happens to be Mercury. For some of you, there may be a chance to travel, which comes completely out of the blue, which leaves you temporarily lost for words, but not for long; you're always quick to take a chance on some kind of adventure, and today is no exception. For other Rams, inspirations will certainly bring admiration for you on the working front, so don't be afraid to voice your thoughts.

SATURDAY 14th You seem to be in something of a confused state, so it's important that you remember there is no such thing as a 'pay off' where emotional investments are concerned. It's important today that you put human relationships first and everything else, including cash, will fall into place over the next couple of days or so. There's more than one way of being rich, and this you'll find out by placing other people's needs ahead of your own for a change.

SUNDAY 15th   You're in an unusually unselfish mood but don't take this too far; remember you are Aries and are supposed to make a few waves of your own on occasions, particularly now if you don't want to be swamped by other people's never-ending demands. Those who rely on you in any way, must be made to understand that it is time for them to think about being independent and, also, that if they keep saying things are going to be bad, then there's a good chance that they may be.

MONDAY 16th   Try to stay resilient today, and above all else don't be surprised if other people withdraw promises or commitments they made to you some time ago. Wait until tomorrow before you finalize cash or work matters. This may be difficult because your patience is already wearing thin, but the longer you delay the more likely you are to get what you want.

TUESDAY 17th   Your ruling planet, Mars, lines up with Neptune today, softening your approach to life and to other people in general. Certainly, you couldn't have a better day if your job relies on imagination, because ideas flood out before you have a chance to stem the tide. This evening is a wonderful time for romance, but if you find yourself with a new admirer, use your intuition because it will tell you whether or not this is the right person for you – or whether it's simply a case of 'okay for now'.

WEDNESDAY 18th   Today, the stars advise you to wait a while before speaking your mind; it looks as if you have a difficult choice to make between family and work. You won't go far wrong if you try to cultivate a little contentment, difficult for you I will admit, but surely you can muster up some for this 24-hour period.

THURSDAY 19th   Today, Mars enters your opposite sign of Libra and so you're certainly not going to be bored in any of your relationships over the next few weeks or so. What's more, you'll be more prepared to put extra effort into a love affair in order to make it work, where normally you would run away at the first sign of difficulty. If you're already married or engaged, don't be surprised if your opposite number suddenly becomes wildly impulsive, highly sexed and passionate about their opinions. You may experience a few battles during this period but you'll eventually win the war and that's the important thing.

FRIDAY 20th   Today is the day of the Full Moon and it occurs in your sign, a clear indication that it is a far better day for putting the finishing touches to work, and even relationships, rather than starting anything new. Try to be as polite as possible when in the company of strangers otherwise it won't take long before you find yourself involved in pitched battle; quite frankly you don't need this kind of aggravation.

SATURDAY 21st   The Sun, in a dodgy aspect with Mars today, could completely ruin your sense of judgement, it's likely you'll be ridiculously over-optimistic or fail to consider all the implications of a decision you want to make. Don't allow other people to force you into a corner and make you promise something that you secretly know you cannot possibly fulfil. If you do, repercussions will be felt for some time to come.

SUNDAY 22nd   Today will help you to free yourself from unrewarding or pricey ties and move easily into a new way of life. So, believe those who come into your life are there by order of fate and remind yourself that the most important thing of all is not to be afraid of taking risks. Usually, you don't think about doing so but, right now, you're being overly cautious.

MONDAY 23rd   If you're a typical Ram, there's nothing you like better than new challenges or change, but even you may find it difficult to cope with some of the outrageous suggestions your friends or contacts are making at this time. You may have to pinch yourself to make sure that you're not dreaming and, when you discover you aren't, it will be a time for trying to talk some common sense into somebody else. This is a switch if ever there was one.

TUESDAY 24th   It would be nice, you feel, if, just for once, those who are supposed to be your loved ones tried to find out why you're in such a negative mood. Someone, somewhere, is about to do just that and make you aware that being human is difficult, becoming human is a lifelong and arduous process, and to be truly human is the greatest gift of all.

WEDNESDAY 25th   The Sun is struggling against a difficult aspect from Pluto. This means that you must fight hard for concentration and also avoid unnecessary change, even if you may be feeling a little bored. Try to maintain the 'status quo' until this mood wears off and you are able to see the proverbial wood for the trees.

THURSDAY 26th   Before you can honestly relax and say that you're 'on your way', you must check everything twice, as it would appear you have missed something along the way. Having done this, treat yourself with respect, kindness and consideration, and remember that, for you anyway, the fun is generally in the struggle and not in the prize.

FRIDAY 27th   The Moon is in your Sign, today, making

you more open-minded to the ideas and suggestions of other people. What's more, you will be reacting to situations from the heart instead of your busy head, and other people will appreciate the fact that you have a heart that's as strong as your will of iron. Make sure you're out and about this evening because you are at your most attractive.

SATURDAY 28th Today, Venus moves into the fiery sign of Leo, which is the romantic as well as artistic and fun side of life. You're in for a few weeks when you can really relax, forget about your troubles and push ahead with the intensely personal side of life. This is certainly a great period for the professional sportsperson or the artist; you, too, can make your strongest desires come true.

SUNDAY 29th This is a time when ideally you should keep your social and travel plans down to a minimum and be certain to place your own welfare and well-being first on your list of priorities. Where money is concerned, you have everything to gain and nothing to lose by keeping your options well and truly open.

MONDAY 30th Whether you're in a relationship or fancy-free, you certainly seem to be counting the cost of believing that other people have the best intentions in the world, and what takes place today could very well be the final straw. On one thing you can be sure, your family is 100 per cent behind you so it's nice to know that you're not completely on your own.

JULY

TUESDAY 1st Venus' aspect with Pluto is certainly useful for those of you who work in big business or need to have dealings with such people. It won't do your love life any harm either, though don't expect everything to run according to plan, because there will be changes to your relationships and in the general atmosphere between yourself and other people.

WEDNESDAY 2nd   See what you can do to make sure that you stay on the right side of your boss and anybody in a position of authority. However, looking slightly further into the future, in a couple of weeks the stars will change the picture completely. You obviously have some kind of grand plan at the ready and will be able to put it into operation soon. In the meantime do try hard to stay patient.

THURSDAY 3rd   Your ruling planet, Mars, is in a wonderful aspect with Uranus and so you certainly have a great deal of personal power. Others will be tripping over their own feet in an effort to impress you and, whilst initially this may amuse, you'd be wise to gather your wits and be ready to take advantage, particularly if you want any kind of favour or if you want to further a romance. Remember, all you've got to do today is to ask and, in the main, it should be granted.

FRIDAY 4th   Today is the day of the New Moon and it occurs in the watery sign of Cancer. If you've any difficulty, either with relatives or property affairs, this is the time for starting anew, once, of course, you have sat down and thrashed things through with other people. If you have decided to invite a few friends around, this evening, either for a drink or a meal, you're going to find them great company. As always, New Moons can be used for pushing ahead into life and you mustn't hesitate to do so.

SATURDAY 5th   Venus is in a quarrelsome mood with Uranus and so it would be a good idea for you to stay as independent as you usually are, because other people are cranky, disagreeable and may spring unpleasant surprises. Romantically, things are sure not to go according to plan and you'll need to dredge up some adaptability from somewhere in order to cope.

SUNDAY 6th Mercury is in a difficult aspect with Neptune, today, and this could make you forgetful. If you keep a diary, for heaven's sake double-check and find out where you're supposed to be and at what time, and make sure that you aren't late because others won't be very pleased. This applies especially if you have an important date this evening with somebody new; to leave them hanging around would antagonize them from the word go.

MONDAY 7th The Moon is in the fiery sign of Leo and that's fine by you because this happens to reflect the pleasure-seeking, romantic and creative sides of life. In these areas you can confidently push ahead in the sure knowledge that you're going to be successful. If you happen to be a parent, it's a good day for making decisions on behalf of the younger members of your family.

TUESDAY 8th Today, Mercury moves into Leo and, while you are normally a very physical person, particularly in your spare time, now it's likely that you may be more attracted to intellectual pursuits. If you happen to be a parent, this is a great time for trying to communicate with children, particularly if they are teenagers because they are more willing to be led by you, for a change.

WEDNESDAY 9th The Moon is in the earthy sign of Virgo and so this could provide you with a couple of days when physically you will easily tire. Ensure that you don't take on anything which is sure to run you ragged; stick to routine and, above all else, see if you can get in a couple of early nights. This certainly won't do you any harm for a change.

THURSDAY 10th You're still feeling a little weary, but you will find that workmates are more than happy to take on extra responsibility, should it become necessary. Don't always imagine that you are completely indispensable because if you do, you could find out the hard way that this simply isn't true. This could provide you with a nasty shock! It's a good day for those of you who are going for any kind of dental or health check-up.

FRIDAY 11th The Sun is lining up with Jupiter and so, when it comes to travel matters, you may be a little careless or forgetful. If you are leaving for any kind of trip, for heaven's sake check out your passport and your luggage, because you may have forgotten something that you simply cannot do without. Other Rams will be thinking big thoughts, but people will be pointing out that you have completely forgotten to consider all the little details, as usual.

SATURDAY 12th The Sun is lining up with Saturn, today, and this suggests that you are overly ambitious, prepared to walk over other people and, not only that, drag your heels as you do. Remember, those you call friends today, could very well turn out to be enemies tomorrow. Do whatever you can to keep others sweet, because nobody is an island, as the old saying goes, and this is a real truism.

SUNDAY 13th Jupiter lines up with Saturn, and, although there might be a slowing down with your plans, this will eventually work to your advantage, although you may not be able to see this for the time being. If you want a discussion with people who are in positions of power or authority, now is the time to try to get them to one side, they'll be receptive to you.

MONDAY 14th Venus lines up with Saturn and this

suggests there could be a serious development in one of your relationships. What you imagine to be a casual flirtation, or maybe even 'a one night stand' proves to be nothing of the sort and this could prove to be something of a shock to your system. Never mind, I can think of worse ways of being surprised and I'm sure you can too. If you've decided to become engaged, you've certainly picked an excellent time.

TUESDAY 15th   Mercury lines up with your ruler, Mars, today, and so concentration flies completely out of the window. The best thing to do is to apply yourself to work, which you can do almost with your eyes shut, rather than trying to take on a new challenge, because you could make a complete hash of it. This, of course, would damage your pride and a depressed Ram is not a pretty sight.

WEDNESDAY 16th   The Moon is in the fiery and adventurous sign of Sagittarius today, making it an ideal time for dealing with people who are abroad or foreigners who may be in your life. The much more adventurous will be reaching out into life like a small child attempting to grab exactly what it wants. Providing you're prepared to make a few allowances, you should be able to achieve your aims.

THURSDAY 17th   If you are in serious doubt about a decision that others seem to be pushing you to make, look back to the past, because it is there that you'll find the answer. Naturally, as a child of the present, you find this hard to do but this is one of the lessons that most Rams have to learn at some point and you may as well start now.

FRIDAY 18th   Mars, at the zenith of your chart in the earthy sign of Capricorn, brings about the strong desire for you to occupy centre stage and push ahead with all your ambitions. Even so, you must remember that you will need to take into consideration the wishes of those in superior positions; you simply can't push ahead regardless of other people and, if you do, you could be storing up a great deal of difficulty for yourself in the future.

SATURDAY 19th   Mercury is in a wonderful aspect with Saturn and so you will be coasting through the day's workload effortlessly. It's a great time if you want to make any sort of professional change, or if you are going on an interview or to an important meeting. It is not a time then for keeping your ambitions to yourself, after all, others can't give you a helping hand unless they know exactly where you want to go.

SUNDAY 20th   The Full Moon, today, occurs at the zenith of your chart so it's lucky it is a Sunday and only some of you will be working. Those who do will meet up with complication after complication. If you are at home, use this time for deciding exactly what your next move should be and, if you are in doubt, go to somebody who can help you iron out all those fiddling little details. On no account mix business with pleasure because it'll be a big disappointment.

MONDAY 21st   The Sun is in a difficult aspect with Neptune today, so don't take anything for granted; no situation or person you meet will be as they seem, in fact others may be actively out to deceive you and, because you are such a trusting soul, you're easily taken in. Those of you who have decided to make a major purchase have certainly picked the wrong time but if you must, do a lot of double-checking, otherwise you may not get value for money.

TUESDAY 22nd   Venus lines up with Neptune today

and so, where yesterday you were creating most of the muddle, on this particular day it is other people who are at fault. You'll save yourself a great deal of agony if you double-check any arrangements you have with them, because they will either have forgotten where they're supposed to be or at what time. You may be tempted to give a really good ticking off to various people, but remember that perhaps they have problems of their own and can't always put their own wants and desires first; unlike you who invariably seems able to do so.

WEDNESDAY 23rd   Today, the Sun moves into the regal sign of Leo and so you are beginning the fun part of the year. Workwise, it's a productive time for those who are involved with children, the arts and sport. Personally, if you are single, that's the way you'll want to stay because there seem to be so many goodies on display; how could you possibly be expected to make a decision! If, on the other hand, you are already in a relationship, watch yourself because flirtatious behaviour could land you in hot water.

THURSDAY 24th   Today, Venus enters the earthy sign of Virgo, which will certainly be throwing a rosy glow over relationships with people you meet whilst going about your professional duties. Healthwise, there'll be a strong tendency for you to indulge in excesses, any little excuse will do, even the cat's birthday. Try to control this, not necessarily for slimming purposes, rather think of the possible damage you're doing to your stomach and other organs.

FRIDAY 25th   The Sun is lining up with Pluto today and it's certainly a day for making sweeping changes in your life. It's hard to imagine you getting through this period without bringing one chapter of life to an end, or launching out in a new direction. Yes, the pioneer within you is definitely on the rampage and so other people will have to make some rapid adjustments for you.

SATURDAY 26th You seem to be raring to go but undoubtedly there are some situations where your hands are tied and you are on dependent on others to help you to get your wishes off the launching pad. An important contract or business opportunity is gathering steam but you must not let your hunger for security place you in a position which has all the trappings of success, but little scope for personal fulfilment.

SUNDAY 27th Mercury moves into Virgo today and this will certainly help those of you who are involved with legal matters, paperwork, or travel. Life will be less fraught than it has been of late and you'll be giving a good account for yourself. The only difficulty is that you will be inclined to tire a little easily, that roaring furnace of yours is down to a flickering flame, so try to pace yourself, attend to everything that has top priority and leave what can be left to one side for the time being.

MONDAY 28th Don't be surprised at the stars today, which point in a direction you feel disinclined to take. You are a competitive person, but you also have a tremendous desire to learn, and at some stage, very soon, you'll discover something – a theory, a belief – that answers many of the questions you have been asking.

TUESDAY 29th Venus lines up with Uranus today and so there is an unexpected and surprising feel about finances as well as your intensely personal relationships. Greet the day with an open mind, ready for literally anything. Luckily, you are able to think on your feet and so even the stars can't catch you up, you're far too speedy for them.

WEDNESDAY 30th The Moon in Gemini may make it

difficult for you to concentrate and so, wherever possible, shelve major decision making and important paperwork for the time being and just tick through the day putting the finishing touches to jobs. This evening, you'll be restless if you stay at home, so get out locally, because it's possible that you'll meet new faces through your friends and you'll be widening your circle as a result.

THURSDAY 31st The Moon is in the domestic sign of Cancer so you're provided with a rare couple of days when you'll derive a great deal of enjoyment from home and family; well, even you need to charge your batteries from time to time. This is a good day if you happen to be trying to push ahead with property matters and, if you really find yourself at a loose end this evening, get on the phone and ask a friend or neighbour around for a drink and a bit of a gossip. Perhaps it's time you caught up with all the local scandal.

AUGUST

FRIDAY 1st There seems to be plenty of change and news in connection with relatives. Some of this may take you aback, so it must be something spectacular, because it takes a great deal to shock a Ram. There may be little you can do about the situation because other people, just like you, have to learn from their own mistakes.

SATURDAY 2nd You're the sort of person who is generally highly organized in everything from your love life to your professional life. However, sometimes fate has a way of turning our plans upside down and it's then that you tend to feel a little put out. The best thing you can do is dredge up some adaptability from somewhere today, because you're certainly going to need it and look upon what happens, completely out of the blue, as a chance to prove just how resilient you can be.

SUNDAY 3rd Today is the day of the New Moon, making it an ideal time for making decisions in connection with artistic work, children, or romance. Pleasure-seeking can be great fun, too, and it's likely many of you will be taking on a new hobby or, alternatively, finding yourself in environments you have never visited before. Never mind, this should appeal to the sense of adventure inside you.

MONDAY 4th The atmosphere could be a little tense today but the Leo Moon will help to melt away worries. If you're hoping to finalize some kind of transaction, or seal an important deal, now is not necessarily the time; forget impulsive behaviour. Something which happens today will prompt second thoughts and, until you are satisfied you have covered every angle, wait a little longer where important matters are concerned.

TUESDAY 5th The Moon in Virgo places the emphasis on your relationship with workmates which can be improved, believe it or not. Possibly someone at your place of employment has been getting on your nerves recently and, if so, now is a good time for sitting down and discussing your differences. You may discover there are no differences whatsoever.

WEDNESDAY 6th The Moon in Virgo is always a good time for attending to your own physical well-being so, if you have been feeling under the weather, now is the time for doing something constructive about this. It is, of course, entirely possible that you have been overdoing it – so what's new! If this is so, take some time out for yourself and do whatever it takes to calm those jangling nerves.

THURSDAY 7th The Moon in Libra could be bringing about changes in at least one of your important emotional relationships. While things are in such a state of flux, it wouldn't be a good idea to make commitments which you may have to retract at a later date. So, control your impulsive head, it could lead you into trouble.

FRIDAY 8th There's a strong possibility that you'll be meeting many new people at this time, which is fine by you because you are one of the most sociable signs of the zodiac. However, do be sure that you don't deliberately go out of your way to cultivate somebody because they might be useful to you; such heartless behaviour could certainly bruise somebody's sensitivity.

SATURDAY 9th The Sun is in a difficult aspect with Jupiter today and, because of this, your judgement goes completely out of the window. You'll certainly be feeling vital and exuberant, but also a little careless; possessions could go astray and you may forget appointments. It might be a good idea to double-check where you're supposed to be and at what time, in order to avoid upsetting other people.

SUNDAY 10th Your ruling planet, Mars, is lining up with Neptune so, where you are normally one of the most highly organized people in the zodiac, this certainly isn't true on this particular day. You become woolly headed and forgetful and may insist on relying on your hunches, even though they are likely to lead you astray. Wherever possible use common sense and you'll get through the day without any kind of mishap.

MONDAY 11th There's every possibility that you'll be able to dispose of any lingering doubts about the viability of a connection or a contract. In fact, you are probably ready to sign on the dotted line. By now, there is a raucous and energetic feel about your relationships; it could be a case of high spirits after a rather difficult patch.

TUESDAY 12th Today, the Sun is lining up with Saturn

and so you are at your most ambitious; heaven help anybody who gets in your way, they will be swept away by a grand gesture. It's always important to remember though, that if you tread on people's toes on your way up, you could very well run into the same people on your way down; so try to be as friendly and as accommodating as possible whilst you fight to establish yourself or show your true worth.

WEDNESDAY 13th   Luckily, Pluto has now decided to resume direct movement so, where official or bureaucratic matters are concerned, life should be a good deal smoother from now on. If you've had any kind of run-in with your bank manager, you will find him or her far easier to approach and much more open-minded to your ideas and suggestions. The bank may even be quite willing to provide some kind of backing for you.

THURSDAY 14th   Mars moves into the watery sign of Scorpio, and you temporarily take on some of the characteristics of this sign, becoming more intense, jealous, and even highly sexed. Well, you've got to take the good with the bad I'm afraid! Even so, those who are closest to you may wonder what on earth has come over you, but, in most cases, will welcome the greater sincerity which seems to be in operation.

FRIDAY 15th   Today, Venus is lining up with Neptune and so other people are positively inspired; if you can force yourself, why don't you sit back and pick their brains because their ideas are certainly going to be much more imaginative than your own. Romantically, this could be a red-letter day, especially if you have something important to celebrate; if not, make something up! Such as the goldfish's birthday!

SATURDAY 16th   The Moon is at the zenith of your chart

and when this happens you invariably keep a very high profile where work matters are concerned. It's a good time for making minor adjustments to your ambitions, but not a time for forging ahead regardless of the opinions and advice coming to you from other people. There's no doubt that you are something of a loner and none of us can survive without the influence of other people for very long I'm afraid.

SUNDAY 17th   Today, Mercury decides to be stupid and goes into retrograde movement which means it appears to be going backwards. Paperwork, documents and travel could all be unbelievably complicated during the next couple of weeks and, if it is necessary for you to involve yourself in these areas of life, do a lot of double-checking.

MONDAY 18th   The Full Moon occurs in the friendship area of your chart and so, unwittingly, other people who mean a great deal to you may let you down. What you must remember is that this is unavoidable and they are not going out of their way to be difficult. Try to be generous and open-minded.

TUESDAY 19th   Today, Venus lines up with Pluto and so there seems to be a sudden upheaval or change, in connection with both cash and the intensely personal side of life. Mind you, if you happen to be completely fancy-free, make sure that you're out and about this evening, looking your best, because you never know! Anyone new who does enter your life will occupy it for some time to come.

WEDNESDAY 20th   Venus moves into your opposite sign of Libra today and, whilst it squats in this sign, which is for a few weeks now, there will be a rosy glow and plenty of harmony in all your close relationships, professional and otherwise. Certainly, if you're fancy-free, you're sure to be bumping into someone really special. And, if you're in a relationship, you may be prepared to take it a step further. If you've decided to become engaged or married during this time, you've been very clever indeed.

THURSDAY 21st   The Moon enters your own sign, so clearly it's a period for drawing attention to your own talents, not that you're ever slow to do so, as a rule. Be prepared, though, to make a few changes; if other people come up with good ideas, don't be offended, take them on, because they can improve on that master plan of yours and make it even more viable and profitable.

FRIDAY 22nd   Neptune today cosies up to the Sun, so don't expect things to run according to plan, they never do when this particular planet is on the go. Double-check anything which is important to you in order to avoid confusion. And don't be surprised if your emotions are in something of a turmoil, because it won't take much to reach the tender heart which is lurking within your breast.

SATURDAY 23rd   Today, the Sun enters the earthy sign of Virgo and so you begin a period of about one month when it is necessary to get down to hard work, without necessarily expecting plenty of praise or attention. It's a good time though for those of you involved in the medical profession, or careers connected with service and health, and for other Rams who wish to deal with such people. Your life is also likely to be more intertwined with those you meet at work, and, in the long-run, you'll be getting a good deal closer to them.

SUNDAY 24th   Today, your ruling planet, Mars, lines up with Uranus, so you're in a rebellious, cranky and unpredictable frame of mind. This is all very well, but why don't you consider the feelings of those closest to you. You may enjoy wreaking havoc, much like a small child does, but unfortunately nobody can command you adult Rams, well not without World War Three breaking out.

MONDAY 25th   Today, the Sun lines up in a difficult aspect with Pluto and, because of this, you may experience a distinct feeling that you are being blocked in at least one area of life. There is no point in banging your head against a brick wall; wait for this influence to pass and, in the meantime, put the finishing touches to those many unfinished projects which are lying around. The same advice applies emotionally; don't push, because, if you do, somebody may leave your life altogether.

TUESDAY 26th   Today, the Moon enters the airy sign of Gemini and this will certainly be keeping you on the go from morning to night, not that you'll mind, of course, because if there's one thing you like to be, it is active. That grey matter is working at full throttle and so paperwork can be dispensed within record time. This evening do get out and about because brief encounters are possible.

WEDNESDAY 27th   Over the next few days the Moon will be in the watery sign of Cancer, a clear signpost from the stars that it is time to turn your attention to your family and their wants and their needs. Too often with you there is a tendency to be 'me first', which is okay for the majority of the time, but now it seems that somebody close to you is hurting through neglect and it's up to you to do something about it. Come on, Aries, where's your big warm heart?

THURSDAY 28th   The emphasis continues to be on the home and property areas of life. If you're looking for a flat, a room or even a house, you could strike gold at this time. Conversely, if you are trying to sell, then you should set your asking price and stick to your guns. Those of you who want to entertain at home this evening will have picked a great time for doing so.

FRIDAY 29th   You're beginning to resent the amount of time that you have had to give to the family side of life, but you've only one more day of this, so hang on in there, Aries, because soon you can get out into life once more and play the pioneer that you are. In the meantime, go through your plans for the future and make sure there are no gaping chasms in them, because too often you overlook the fiddling little details.

SATURDAY 30th   The Sun is in the fiery sign of Leo and so you re-enter the social scene in quite a big way. You've mounds of energy at your disposal but it needs to be channelled into something tangible, a strenuous sport perhaps, or in overcoming the next hurdle in your ambitions. It's a good time for trying a new pastime and certainly romance is flirtatious and fun. Not a time for serious, emotional commitments though!

SUNDAY 31st   This may be a Sunday, but you're not about to sit around doing nothing, if you do, your toes will be tapping, your fingers will be drumming and you'll be getting on everybody's nerves. Get out for a brisk walk, contact friends you have neglected for quite some time. If you've a partner give them 100 per cent of your attention, you'll get a great deal back in the way of appreciation, perhaps love-making, so maybe this will provide you with the spur that is much needed on this particular day.

SEPTEMBER

MONDAY 1st   Today, the month starts off with a twinkling New Moon and so you are filled with a good deal of trepidation, as well as enthusiasm, for this particular month. Mind you, you won't get very far unless you are willing to put in a degree of hard work, but be assured that any efforts you do put in will certainly be repaid, financially and also in a form of gratitude, not that you're looking for the latter but you're certainly looking for the former. Those of you who may have been off colour recently should be improving in leaps and bounds.

TUESDAY 2nd People at work seem to be blowing hot and cold and this could have the effect of making you feel like cutting yourself off from them for a while. How you hate to be at the mercy of the whims of other people, but you simply can't force the pace at the moment! Hold tight and refuse to be drawn, or baited, until you are sure of what your next step must be. In the meantime, your plans are taking an exciting shape in your mind.

WEDNESDAY 3rd New introductions widening your circle of contacts combine to lift your social life into a new area. It seems that one avenue is turning out to be a bit of a dead end, so you should take off and explore new directions. Casting your net a little wider will produce all sorts of interesting options.

THURSDAY 4th Your ruling planet, Mars, is in a difficult aspect with Jupiter today, so guard against being over-optimistic, careless, or looking to find the easy way out, because there isn't such a thing, believe me. This evening, you'll be drawn to excesses and, although you may believe that a thumping head or an upset stomach is a good price to pay, I doubt whether you'll say the same thing tomorrow. Shelve important decisions until you can see more clearly.

FRIDAY 5th Right now, you feel determined to win at all costs and, in spite of set-backs, the odds are still in your favour for realizing a particular ambition. Soon, you'll be greatly rewarded for the efforts you are putting in at this time. In the meanwhile, make sure that you're in control of your finances and not that they are in control of you.

SATURDAY 6th It's likely that you may be feeling restless as well as experiencing a need for excitement and maybe even glamour. The stars today will contribute to your desire to be taken away from a pressing workload. Luckily, soon, the stars will allow you the time and chance to indulge yourself, but taking a short cut now could create more work than is actually saved.

SUNDAY 7th Turn your attention to what gives you pleasure in life. Too often, you believe that leisure-time is just another reason for slaving away, but now you're provided with a chance to make a real impact on your close relationships, which also gives you a chance to rebuild your damaged confidence.

MONDAY 8th It's time to do a little double-checking to make sure all your plans and arrangements are watertight. Try hard to keep a sense of proportion even though you may have reason to feel encouraged to go for the highest possible goal. So much is trying to happen at once and this is a time where discrimination and judgement will win the day, rather than biting off more than you can comfortably chew.

TUESDAY 9th You may have to do battle today; the stars suggest it's important for you to find all your courage and determination, which shouldn't be difficult. Remember not to be evasive because it will not get you the long-term answers you need to solve current problems. Be your usual daring and experimental self because it will eventually pay off.

WEDNESDAY 10th Mercury has finally decided to resume direct movement and so contracts, paperwork and travel need hold no fear for you. This is also a time when you can cheerfully line up negotiations and appointments and interviews in the knowledge that you are doing so at the right time when you can maximize your luck.

THURSDAY 11th   The Moon in the fiery sign of Sagittarius is trying to stop you in your tracks and make you think back to past times, because only in this way can you learn from your experiences and put them to good use at this time. This evening, try your hand at something new, you may have got stuck in a rut on the social level and now is the time for branching out.

FRIDAY 12th   Venus moves into the watery sign of Scorpio and this throws a happy glow over the bureaucratic and official channels of life. So, if your life has been made a misery by somebody in this direction, have the confidence to stand up for yourself, particularly if you know you are right and you probably are.

SATURDAY 13th   Your ruling planet, Mars, lines up with Saturn, bringing you down to earth with a thump. This is no bad thing because you will actually be forced do some forward planning and may even be learning from past mistakes. Better mark this down in your diary as a red-letter day because very rarely does this happen; usually you charge ahead regardless of the consequences, but not today.

SUNDAY 14th   So much of what is taking place, right now, is designed to help you drop your old defences and live life as spontaneously as possible. This may mean taking a bigger risk and actually allowing other people to see that you are human after all. Try to be as sociable as you possibly can; don't lock out those who mean the most to you because they'll be nursing feelings of hurt and neglect.

MONDAY 15th   Life really takes you by surprise but

you'll welcome it, because you are able to tune in to the unexpected, particularly at the moment. For a while now, you have been labouring with people who either misunderstand or try to box you in, but you are about to be given a passport to freedom. It's up to you to decide how you're going to use it.

TUESDAY 16th The Full Moon in the sign of Pisces could be a rather unsettling influence. Usually, you're a little ray of sunshine bursting full of confidence, but right now you have serious inner doubts. Whilst this mood continues it's best not to make any important decisions for fear of going off at half-cock. If you do, you'll need to retrace your steps and, as an impatient Aries, you really are loth to do this.

WEDNESDAY 17th It's still a time when you should be feeling your way through situations and relationships, rather than plunging ahead in your usual cavalier fashion. Those of you who work behind the scenes will be doing extremely well right now, because imagination runs riot. In your personal life, somebody may not be as open and honest as you would like but they have their reasons for being secretive and eventually you'll understand.

THURSDAY 18th Venus moves into your opposite sign of Libra casting a rosy, happy glow over all your intimate affairs. Those of you in a relationship will be getting closer to the other person and may even be ready to 'name the day'. If you are a fancy-free Ram, you may strongly fancy a relationship with the intention of 'love them and leave them', but before you know where you are, you're head over heels in love. There are worse things that can happen, you know!

FRIDAY 19th Mercury lines up with Venus and so, like it or not, you are prone to the whims and the fancies of other people at the moment, and you ignore them at your peril. On the working front, the ideas of colleagues will probably outshine yours and you must stifle any feelings of envy. This evening it will pay you to get out and socialize as much as possible, particularly if you're single, because you never know!

SATURDAY 20th   The Sun is in a wonderful aspect with Neptune and so it is your turn to have all the bright ideas and, instead of analysing everything under your gaze, be prepared to go on how you feel, because those intuitions are there for a reason, even if you rarely listen to them. Make this a day of the exception rather than the rule.

SUNDAY 21st   Today, the Moon is in the earthy sign of Taurus which governs the cash area of your life. Because of this, there seems to be a great deal of movement which can only mean that you're in one of your impulse-buying moods. Oh dear! You could do a great deal of damage, so, where possible, stick to buying essentials and even these should be purchased by other people rather than your good self, because you could get carried away.

MONDAY 22nd   Venus is in a difficult aspect with Jupiter today and so it is important that you rely on your own ideas, because other people are not seeing things clearly and are being rather careless and self-indulgent. This evening, you may find yourself trying to help somebody who has perhaps eaten or drunk too much and the responsibility seems to fall on your shoulders, for some reason or other, to make sure that they get home safely. Avoid making important emotional decisions on this day.

TUESDAY 23rd   Today, the Sun moves into the airy sign of Libra which is your opposite sign. Over the next couple of weeks or so, it is important that you learn to share more and consider the ideas and thoughts of other people, because their suggestions will be just as original and as exciting as your own for a change. Professional relationships are also likely to be improving and rivals suddenly become close friends.

WEDNESDAY 24th   The Moon in Cancer suggests that it is time for you to pay attention to what is going on within the family; it's likely that loved ones have been seriously neglected whilst you've been out pioneering your way through life. If you've decided to entertain at home over the next couple of days you've certainly picked the best time. You'll make an excellent host or hostess and will be creating a warm and welcoming atmosphere.

THURSDAY 25th   Your ruling planet, Mars, lines up with Neptune today, putting you in a sentimental and romantic mood. Possibly, something will occur which will take you back in time and you'll spend several hours reminiscing, either quietly on your own or, perhaps, in the company of an old friend you haven't seen for some while. Certainly, if you're in a relationship, the other person will be benefitting, by way of affection and attention.

FRIDAY 26th   The Moon in Leo is likely to bring changes to your long made social arrangements and perhaps also to a date you are looking forward to. No need to get neurotic or insecure if somebody cancels, their reasons are valid and they are not avoiding you, so side-step any tendency to feel persecuted. A great time for those of you who are awaiting news in connection with a creative project.

SATURDAY 27th   The Sun is in a beautiful aspect with Uranus, a time which certainly benefits those of you in a professional partnership or those who are part of a team. On no account should you try to struggle on through life independently, because, whether you like it or not, you need other people, not only for company but also to get their slant on a particular situation which is relevant at this time particularly.

SUNDAY 28th Today, the Sun cuddles up to Pluto so don't expect the day to run smoothly; there may be at least one beginning or ending and, although this may initially throw you, believe me this is all for the best, which you will see and accept with the passage of time. If you want to make any last-minute changes to your social or romantic plans, feel free to do so.

MONDAY 29th You ruling planet, Mars, now enters the sign of Sagittarius and so you'll experience a wonderful few weeks when the emphasis could very well be on improving your mind, long-distance travel or foreign affairs. When it comes to socializing, you are perhaps a little tired of going to the same old haunts with the same old faces and are now reaching out and ready to embrace anything and anyone new. Just make sure, Aries, that when it comes to romance, you don't make the same mistake again because rarely do you learn from the past; try to make this an exception.

TUESDAY 30th The Moon has now moved into the earthy sign of Virgo, an area of your chart devoted to hard graft and also the affairs of your workmates. Instead of treating colleagues as deadly enemies it could be an idea to co-operate with them more, pick their brains and, where necessary, join forces. Try not to overdo the late-night scene this evening because energy is going to run out far quicker than you could possibly imagine.

OCTOBER

WEDNESDAY 1st We have yet another month which begins with a New Moon and this particular one is situated in the sign of Libra. Quite obviously then, your intensely personal relationships certainly are receiving a shot in the arm and there'll be a better understanding between yourself and those who mean the most to you. If you are fancy-free, many of you will start the month with a new romance. What a lovely way to start, but don't rush in where the other eleven Signs would fear to tread; slow down a bit, enjoy the view and get to know this person better before you make up your mind whether you want to become seriously involved.

THURSDAY 2nd There are very few Signs who are as straightforward as you, and this is the very reason why you need to make allowances for other people's behaviour. Right now, there is a theme of change and movement in your circle and people may be reluctant to commit themselves emotionally or even socially. No amount of shouting and screaming will improve the situation, so you may as well smile sweetly, keep yourself busy and wait for them to decide what the next move should be.

FRIDAY 3rd The Moon in Scorpio strongly suggests that you avoid becoming involved in any kind of intrigue, or activity behind the scenes. There are going to be plenty who will promise you whatever you want to hear, if only you will change sides or give them information, but you're not the type to let yourself be bribed. Remember that happiness is not a matter of events, it depends on your frame of mind, so do your best to keep your head free from clutter and you can be as content as you need to be.

SATURDAY 4th Today, Mercury lines up with the charismatic Uranus. Because of this don't expect to stick to routine, not that you are any lover of this particular word. Chances are that there may be an opportunity for you to go on a short trip quite unexpectedly, if not, you'll find little reasons for popping in and out of work and also in and out of your home this evening. You're compelled to keep on the move because you need an array of new faces and exciting atmospheres to keep you stimulated. So, a day full of incident and one particularly lucky for those professionally involved in sales.

SUNDAY 5th After a relatively 'up' start to the month, we now have a difficult day when the Sun is in a compromising position with Saturn. There's a chance that some of you will be feeling over-optimistic where a work or career opportunity is concerned; do keep your feet on the ground until everything has been signed and sealed, which is unlikely to be today. Perhaps the social occasion you were looking forward to may either not come up to your high expectations or may be cancelled altogether, so you need to stay as resilient as you possibly can, and that's a great demand; put your mind to it.

MONDAY 6th Your ruling planet, Mars, is in a wonderful aspect with Uranus today, so literally anything can happen and you're sure to be playing a prominent role in all events. You've loads of good ideas and their originality will impress people at work as well as at home. Friends are willing to help you out and make interesting introductions, so shelve your pride and don't be afraid to ask.

TUESDAY 7th The Moon's position in the fiery sign of Sagittarius suggests that you should stop in your tracks and look back to the past, because there you may find an answer to a current quandary. This isn't easy for you to do because your Sign tends to live firmly in the present rather than in the 'yester-year', even so, the experiences we glean can always be used positively, an astrological lesson you need to learn.

WEDNESDAY 8th Venus moves into Sagittarius today, placing emphasis and a good deal of happiness and luck on matters related to improvement of the mind, foreign affairs and travel. If you work in any of these areas you'll certainly be doing extremely well for yourself and can afford to push your luck. If you're fancy-free, you'll be drawn to those with unusual accents; you certainly have a taste for the exotic right now which is fine providing, of course, you are looking at the person as well as their appearance. Too often you are taken in by superficials.

THURSDAY 9th The Moon in Capricorn makes it a lively day on the working front and you've sufficient energy to cope. In fact, you have enough enthusiasm to drive at least four locomotives and others will be keeling over with exhaustion as you tear through life. Remember, this evening, to slow down a little and enjoy the scenery.

FRIDAY 10th The Sun today is in a nice aspect with Saturn so you couldn't have a better time for making serious decisions or attending to intricate or difficult work. Older people will have some good advice for you; the question is, are you going to listen? I doubt it very much, but you could live to regret the fact that you didn't; so think twice.

SATURDAY 11th Mercury is in a difficult aspect with Saturn today and this may bring you down. There may not be any particular reason, it's just one of those days when you're not feeling your old self and, wherever you go, you feel a little uneasy. The best thing to do is to use your time for sorting out work that has been left incomplete, or simply resting up this evening and recharging your batteries, because they sure need it.

SUNDAY 12th The Moon in the airy sign of Aquarius places the emphasis on your friendships, contacts and acquaintances. It's a good time for club activities, particularly the sporting variety. It's difficult to imagine you staying at home at this time because you're far too motivated and geared up for action. There are romantic possibilities, too, though perhaps they shouldn't be taken too seriously.

MONDAY 13th   The Moon in Pisces provides you with a quiet period of reflection, not that you ever think that you need one. Despite this, we all need to gather our wits occasionally and decide what our next move is going to be and this is your time. Use your instincts when in the company of new people; you'll be sussing them out in record time.

TUESDAY 14th   The Sun is in a lovely aspect with Mercury today and, because of this, it's a good time for signing documents or travelling, especially if it is connected with children or the arts. If you're at home, and the young people there have been difficult to handle, this is the time for sitting them down sensibly and talking things through. Resist any temptation to thump the table or throw your weight around, it won't achieve anything at all.

WEDNESDAY 15th   The Moon is in your Sign today so step into centre stage and gather all the admiration and praise that is waiting for you. This is a great time for making decisions because you are thinking clearly and a little more slowly than is usually the case, and this can be no bad thing. This evening, you'll have various ways to have fun and can afford to sit back and think carefully before making any kind of decision; to rush ahead may mean you lose out.

THURSDAY 16th   Today is the day of the Full Moon which may dampen your spirits during the early part of the day but, luckily, because Mars is lining up with Jupiter, you perk up as the hours speed past. Don't take negative thoughts too seriously during the morning because later on you'll wonder what on earth had come over you. It's a good evening for being adventurous and trying new activities which are alien to you.

FRIDAY 17th While you are inquisitive and sometimes unconventional, you're not the easiest person to convince. Despite this, right now, all partnership affairs can only go from strength to strength, no matter how many harsh words or sulky silences there may have been. Don't just tell loved ones how much you care – show them.

SATURDAY 18th If you have lost heart recently because your efforts to shine have been frustrated by other people's lack of confidence in you, then now, certainly where work is concerned, you seem to be spoiled for choice. Sympathy and understanding are around you, but what is needed is the kind of tenacity which can move mountains a bucketful at a time.

SUNDAY 19th There's an inclination for you to over-react to situations, maybe because you're not exactly at the top of somebody's popularity polls, or you have been told to be more patient. Naturally, you're free to handle this situation in any way you please, but no matter what you do I'm afraid you are going to run into some opposition. Better by far, then, to accept the things you can't change and not place too much importance on the way other people think about you.

MONDAY 20th The Sun today is in a difficult aspect with Neptune; this is likely to slow down your progress, particularly where matters connected with children, creativity and even animals are concerned. Social arrangements in a love affair have become unduly secretive or muddled, so if your arrangements were made some time ago it might be a good idea to get on the phone and double-check, because it's quite likely that other people have forgotten all about them.

TUESDAY 21st   This is a time when others will believe you have thrown caution to the wind and are busy sorting out who is important to you and who is not. What is really needed is a cooling off period, a time to think on why things happened and what they mean for the future; do this before you jettison someone from your life who later you might realize is indispensable.

WEDNESDAY 22nd   Venus is in a comfortable aspect with Saturn today and, because of this, you'll find that those who are closest to you are in a serious and down-to-earth mood. At some point, they may want to discuss future plans with you or work out differences and, instead of dashing through life at your usual breakneck speed, it might be a good idea to sit down, be adult and work out your differences in a practical fashion. Emotionally, if you're single, you may be ready to make a commitment.

THURSDAY 23rd   The Sun today moves into the watery sign of Scorpio, the part of your chart devoted to banking, insurance and also monies that you share with other people. If the person you are involved with has been over-extravagant lately you'll soon be letting them know in your usual Aries direct manner that you're not best pleased. Don't be hypocritical though, Aries, because, let's face it, when it comes to cash you can be as rash as the next person.

FRIDAY 24th   There's now a nice light-hearted feel about today, provided by the Moon in Leo. Certainly, work appears to be routine unless it's artistic, in which case you have that extra flair, but, this aside, you are turning your attention to pleasure and social arrangements. It's a great evening for sports and romance too, though don't take the latter seriously, other people are likely to be in a flirtatious mood.

SATURDAY 25th   Venus is in a beautiful aspect with Mars today, so you're looking and feeling good; it is certainly a great day for forming new relationships. Many of you will decide to make an important commitment and, if you are getting engaged or married at this particular time, you've been a very clever Ram indeed.

SUNDAY 26th   The Moon in Virgo provides you with the time for relaxing, lazing around the house; yes, unusually, you are feeling completely unmotivated and it will probably do you the world of good. Certainly, your loved ones may wonder what on earth has come over you, nevertheless, secretly, they will be appreciating the peace and quiet. Who can blame them!

MONDAY 27th   There's a great deal of movement and change in the lives of your workmates and some of them may be coming to you for advice. Now, Aries, remember that there have been times when they have been 'there' for you, and now it is your to return the favour. Any changes that do take place on the working front will work out well and there's no need for you to feel insecure. Don't make it too late a night; you may run out of steam.

TUESDAY 28th   The Sun is in a difficult aspect with Uranus today, so if you work on a creative level there will be constant interruptions which could cause you stress. Where friends are concerned, they may promise more than they can fulfil. Certainly their intentions are good, they want to help, but circumstances seem to be against them. Best to avoid club activities this evening, they won't be as enjoyable as you might have imagined.

WEDNESDAY 29th   The Moon, today, is in your opposite sign of Libra and this stirs up a certain amount of restlessness, so it's not a good idea to turn your attention to anything which needs a great deal of thought, decision making or brain activity because, if you do, I'm afraid mistakes are a possibility. Just tick through the day, sticking to routine and make sure you get in some rest this evening.

THURSDAY 30th   The Moon continues in Libra but today it's quite likely to bring the need for you to make minor decisions in connection with a relationship. If you are single, there are various attractive propositions paraded in front of your eyes, but don't fall into the temptation of forming multiple relationships because, if you do, this is going to complicate your life unduly in the future; you may think this could be fun but in the end the heartache will prove not to be worth all the trouble.

FRIDAY 31st   The New Moon today occurs in the sign of Scorpio so, if your finances are tied in with somebody else's, he or she could receive something of a boost. This is a time, too, when you should take at least a couple of hours for some deep thought; make the most of it because this doesn't very often occur; use your time to make important decisions; think them through carefully instead of plunging ahead in your usual fashion.

NOVEMBER

SATURDAY 1st   Today, Uranus cuddles up to Pluto and so, where teamwork, friendship and acquaintances are concerned, literally anything can happen. There's no point in trying to foist your ideas on to other people because they'll be having none of it. They've suddenly developed minds of their own and they're not about to be bullied, cajoled or persuaded around to your way of thinking. So, clearly, a day when you must work under your own steam, and this is no bad thing because these are the ideal circumstances under which you are usually able to shine. This evening, even your closest friends could be unpredictable, so if you have long-made plans with them, it might be a good idea to get on the telephone and double-check.

SUNDAY 2nd   This is an ideal time for getting out and about and the further you travel the more at ease you will feel about your life and yourself. Wherever possible, visit friends who live at a distance, because travelling shouldn't present you with any great difficulty and you'll find a warm welcome waiting for you when you get there. You're likely to spend your time chewing over old times; this is sure to evoke a sentimental mood.

MONDAY 3rd   If your work seems to have become rather dull and burdensome, now is the time for adding a 'touch of magic' because you have plenty of original ideas which can turn projects around and make them far more exciting. Don't be afraid to experiment as long as you have the permission of your boss. This evening, spend your time with people who are new to your circle rather than sticking with the same old faces, because you'll become bored with repeated coversations and may find it hard to disguise the way you feel. Somebody's feelings could be hurt.

TUESDAY 4th   You may find it difficult to get started today. Perhaps travelling has been fraught with delay and frustration, so that by the time you get to work you can hardly be described as being in the best of spirits. Nevertheless, as the day wears on, you become your usual organized self and are determined to give some of your more imaginative ideas a bit of an airing. Don't be afraid to do so, because I think you'll find there'll be a warm welcome waiting for them. This evening is an ideal time for mixing business with pleasure.

WEDNESDAY 5th   Today, the Sun is in a difficult aspect

with Jupiter and so, if your work is at all detailed or requires a great deal of concentration, you would be well advised either do some double-checking or turn your attention to something less arduous. Try to avoid making any kind of important decision, professional or personal, because you are not seeing situations as they really are, only how you would like them to be and that is quite a different matter.

THURSDAY 6th There seems to be a good deal of news and gossip flying around at work, but if you're wise, although you may listen you'll dismiss this as hearsay because that is exactly what it is. This evening, you may have difficulty putting aside thorny work problems but you really must try, if only for the sake of those you care about, because, if you look carefully, you'll find their eyes are glazing over and they may find excuses to avoid you, which would be a great pity because you're in the mood for plenty of company.

FRIDAY 7th The Sun is in a difficult aspect with Saturn today and there will be a tendency for you to be too cocksure. There's always a tendency with Aries to become a little arrogant when confidence is running high, but this is not a quality which proves to be attractive to other people, as I'm sure you'll understand. Ensure that you listen to what other people have to say because, remember, their opinions are as valid as your own. Don't let a 'me first' approach make difficulties; it will be only too easy for this to happen.

SATURDAY 8th This is certainly a sociable day, one when you can make new friends, visit clubs or get together with your older companions and chew over problems and worries. Romantically, it's certainly better for those already in a relationship, because, if you're fancy-free although, others may be in a flirtatious mood, they are likely to have somebody else tucked away at home, and you're not the type to involve yourself in any kind of deceit.

SUNDAY 9th   Ideally, you should make this a quiet day because you need time to replenish your energy which seems to be slowly deserting you. Don't feel guilty about putting your feet up and indulging yourself, it won't do any harm, occasionally, and besides, it'll give everybody else the chance to occupy centre stage and let you know how they feel about life instead of constantly listening to your opinions, which though interesting can become a little wearisome on occasions.

MONDAY 10th   Mercury is in a lovely aspect with Pluto today and so if you need to deal with officials, the taxman or your bank manager, you won't have any problem in persuading them around to your way of thinking. However, your thought patterns are erratic! Usually you make up your mind in ten seconds flat and are generally spot on; now you can see the many shades of grey between black and white and this can be no bad thing, because it will help you to be more fair-minded.

TUESDAY 11th   Today, Mercury lines up with Uranus and you are positively inspired, but there is no point in coming up with brilliant suggestions if you don't follow them up. So, sit down, work everything out in detail because it is only when you have done so that you will impress the people you approach. This evening, there's plenty of news and action in your circle of friends and you could find romance whilst you're visiting a club, so be prepared to kick up your heels and have fun.

WEDNESDAY 12th   The Moon is in your Sign, so you'll be bathing in the spotlight. The only trouble is you must make sure that you don't impose your ideas and opinions on other people; remember they are free-thinking humans, too, and may have a completely different slant on life and its problems. If you are to have a peaceful day, you'll give them a listen and perhaps then reach a happy compromise.

THURSDAY 13th   The Sun is in the earthy sign of Taurus today and this falls in the cash area of your chart. There's a great deal of coming and going in this direction so it looks as if one of those crazy extravagant moods of yours has you in its grip. There's no reason at all why you can't spend on necessities, and even treat yourself, modestly, but if you're going to behave as if there is no limit to your bank account, then you're going to be paying for it at a later date.

FRIDAY 14th   Today is the Full Moon and it occurs in the cash area of life; you need to be careful, particularly where your possessions are concerned. You could spend a frustrating two or three hours searching for something of value, becoming more frustrated and angry as the time passes. As always, Full Moons are wonderful for putting the finishing touches to things and you must remember that, although you are great at initiating affairs, frequently you don't follow them up; this doesn't happen to be the case at the moment so you can turn this Full Moon around and make it really work for you, providing you act in the appropriate fashion.

SATURDAY 15th   Jupiter lines up with Saturn today, so there could definitely be an upswing in your affairs. Those of you who have decided to socialize with workmates will find them great company and, if you are fancy-free, they'll even be introducing you to a potential new romance. It's a great time for travelling, although do make allowances for a certain amount of delay; if you leave everything to the last minute you're going to finish up highly frustrated, ranting and raving, and probably hurting your fellow travel companions.

SUNDAY 16th Right now you have a head bursting full of ideas, but when haven't you? This is all well and good, but what you must accept is that some of them will be positively brilliant but most of them will probably either lack substance or be totally impractical. Once you can accept this fact, you'll be able to sift through your inspirations, chuck out the dross and make the most of what happens to be viable; certainly others will be prepared to listen to you if they think you've done your homework.

MONDAY 17th Mercury is lining up with sensible Saturn and so you're very well-grounded today; instead of revolving your entire conversation and thoughts around yourself, you're prepared to be a little more thoughtful and considerate of others. This will be earning you a great deal in the way of 'Brownie points' and you may even be receiving some invitations for future entertainment. At work, you will instinctively know what needs to be done, how and when, and the hours will positively speed past.

TUESDAY 18th The Moon is in the watery sign of Cancer, suggesting, whether you listen or not, that it is about time you spent some time either in the company of your family or at least listening to what they have to say. It's likely that you've been so preoccupied with your own thoughts and ambitions that loved ones have been sadly neglected; if so, now is the time to rush in there, as only you can, and do a quick rescue job. If you're entertaining at home you'll certainly be gaining a great deal of admiration. Well, with your style how could you not!

WEDNESDAY 19th Today, the Sun is lining up with

hazy and dreamy Neptune. Because of this, you really must make sure of your facts before you make suggestions to other people, either at work or on the home front. You're in need of a great deal of affection this evening and should go wherever you think you can find it. If you're completely fancy-free, your single status may be bothering you at the moment but don't allow this to lead you into forming relationships with literally anybody simply, because you are frightened of being left on the shelf.

THURSDAY 20th Venus and Saturn are at odds with one another right now and, because of this, you may find that other people are a little depressive and even negative; this is sure to make you impatient, you can never understand how people can always look on the dark side of things when you can only see the bright and the positive. Instead of tearing your hair out, why not give them a little encouragement, maybe some flattery, you'll find either or both will work wonders. Yes, Aries, it's time to give to other people and, if you can bring yourself to do so, your day will not have been wasted.

FRIDAY 21st You're in a mood for throwing caution to the wind and breaking out of relationships which don't seem to be contributing a great deal to your life. Before you do, though, it might be a good idea to take a cooling off period, a time to reflect on why events have occurred in the way they have and what they mean for the future. It's a good time for polishing up your many talents.

SATURDAY 22nd No matter how difficult you may find life on occasions, remember the planets are always moving and fresh influences constantly come in to play. Although you'll find it difficult to believe, if you think hard you'll find many reasons to feel optimistic about the future. In the past, where others have blocked your progress, they will now do everything they can to help you out and make you feel important.

SUNDAY 23rd   You may find yourself confused by the attitude of loved ones, you may even view the future with a certain amount of hesitancy, for a change. But is it really as bad as you think? Certainly your bank account might be suffering, just a little, but it's likely that you have everything out of proportion. If you do a little careful homework, I think you'll find that everything will be falling into place.

MONDAY 24th   If you have recently experienced the feeling that your best-laid plans have not turned out the way you expected, then you'll be glad to hear that from now on your progress is going to be quite spectacular. You may have waited quite a while to receive what you deserve on the cash front, but the longer you wait the more worthwhile it's likely to be, so try to bear this in mind.

TUESDAY 25th   Your inner enemy today, unusually so, is excessive caution. The planets will give you a chance to put a romantic, marital or social relationship on a better footing but, because Saturn is now moving backwards through your sign, you may be worried about doing so. Don't be afraid. The doubts holding you back are in your imagination. Hesitate too long and a chance may disappear.

WEDNESDAY 26th   This looks as if it's going to be one of those days when no amount of explanation will help you to get your point across. In fact, the more you defend yourself the worse the situation seems to become. In every respect this is a day in which actions can and must speak louder than words.

THURSDAY 27th   The Sun is in a friendly aspect with

Uranus today and, because of this, you'll find that friends, acquaintances and contacts are all willing to be of help to you. All you have to do is shelve your pride and not be afraid to ask, for fear of losing face. Remember, Aries, you may be self-motivated but even so, you, like everybody else, need other people sometimes and this is one of those occasions. This evening, you could do worse than visit a club because there is a strong possibility of romance if you happen to be fancy-free. If you're in a relationship, why not ask friends, who live close by, to pop in and see you – they'll brighten up your evening?

FRIDAY 28th   The Sun lines up with Pluto today. Because of this, no amount of bullying or threatening behaviour, especially from official sources, will be allowed to undermine your confidence. You'll be standing your ground and putting in a good account of yourself and, to your surprise, your words prove to be extremely effective. This evening, do double-check all long-standing arrangements because other people may very well have forgotten; difficult though it is to imagine anybody overlooking you, Aries, but it can happen when little emergencies arise, as they do from time to time.

SATURDAY 29th   The Moon is in the fiery sign of Sagittarius so, although it's a good time for travelling, it is also a great one for taking on new interests and relationships. If you have a thorny problem that's been hanging around for a considerable while now, take a couple of hours to think back to past experience because, in doing so, you will find the answer to this difficulty. You're at your most outgoing this evening and this is sure to draw the attention of others.

SUNDAY 30th   The New Moon today rounds off the month nicely. You're in a very adventurous mood and the only blot on the horizon will be if somebody insists that you stay close at hand on the home front. You must insist, gently, that they join you in some new-found pastime, or perhaps introduce them to a recently made friend or acquaintance. As always, with New Moons, it's a great time for fresh beginnings, changes of attitude and maybe, if you're really lucky, somebody will be getting in touch just as you were thinking about them – strange how this sometimes happens, isn't it?

DECEMBER

MONDAY 1st During the morning, you are likely to be in something of a dreamy mood. Perhaps something has happened which has taken your mind back to the past, and so you find it difficult to force yourself into concentrating on matters at hand. Be on your guard against making mistakes. Luckily, once the day wears on, you are able to rush around and make up for lost time; it's likely, too, that you'll be keeping a high profile on the working front and other people will be hanging on your every word. Keep in the limelight, this evening, because you could be attracting in a big way and you, more than anybody else, would hate to miss out by playing the shrinking violet; an extremely unlikely event!

TUESDAY 2nd You may have some brilliant ideas on how you can step up efficiency at your place of work, but you need to choose your time carefully before presenting them to other people. To simply push ahead, on the spur of the moment, as you usually do, will only make you unpopular. So, sit down quietly, wait for the right opportunity and then be quick to grab it with both hands. This evening, you may find it difficult to resist discussing your ambitions; don't bore everybody with your working problems.

WEDNESDAY 3rd   It's important that you keep a sense of perspective. Right now, there is a tendency for you to think only of yourself, your ambitions or your work and ignore the wants and the needs of those who are closest to you. If you keep this current mood running for any length of time, you're going to be very unpopular and may also find yourself on the receiving end of somebody else's sharp tongue. This particular evening is an ideal time for asking a few friends around for a drink, or a meal, because you are at your most sociable and so are those you live with.

THURSDAY 4th   Uranus lines up with Pluto, so it won't pay you to assume automatically that everybody is going to run around and give you support. Put your toe in the water first and, if it isn't bitten off, you may be able to afford to take the plunge. Don't be surprised if this evening long-made plans suddenly bite the dust. There's no point in getting hot under the collar about this; unexpected happenings occur in all our personal lives and this certainly seems to be the case, right now; so make some allowances.

FRIDAY 5th   The Sun is in a beautiful aspect with Saturn today and this seems to signify that you are certainly on the right track when it comes to a professional ambition. This evening looks set fair for romance and you seem to have decided to slow down to a decent trot instead of tearing around trying to cram in as much activity as possible. In doing so, you may suddenly notice that somebody is showing either a sexual or emotional interest in you, and you'll now be provided with a chance to do something constructive about this.

SATURDAY 6th   Although Saturn in your Sign continues to warn you not to take romance too much for granted, on balance, there should be fewer disagreements now. You are at last able to focus on things you have in common with others, rather than the things that keep you apart. Naturally, there's no way you can rewrite the past, but you're unlikely to want to, because the future seems to look so bright.

SUNDAY 7th   Jupiter is now travelling through the area of your chart related to hopes, wishes and friendships. No doubt, someone already has brought out the best in you, or is about to. It's no real exaggeration to say that the stars will reverse all the negative trends of recent weeks and repay you in kind for all your caring, trust and faith in human nature.

MONDAY 8th   Today, the Moon is in your Sign and, because of this, you should feel free to step into the spotlight and let other people know exactly how you're feeling and what you are thinking. Don't overdo it, though, because there's a distinct tendency in you to be a little boastful, particularly when you get on to your favourite subject, namely, yourself. Remember that other people have wants and needs, too, and it is about time, perhaps, that you did something constructive about this. This evening, you are more emotional than is usually the case and so somebody will be receiving a good deal in the way of warmth and affection.

TUESDAY 9th   Venus is lining up with mystical and romantic Neptune. This suggests that those who are closest to you are at their most vulnerable and sensitive, so don't override their feelings; also try to remember if this date has any particular significance, because if it has, and you forget, somebody is going to be deeply hurt. If you're fancy-free, make sure that you keep a high profile this evening, because romance is definitely written in the stars. Whether it is long-lasting is something else, but you don't worry about that because, as always, you live in the moment. Mind you, you must consider other people's feelings and if your intentions are anything but honourable, it might be considerate to point this fact out in some tactful way.

WEDNESDAY 10th The Sun lines up with Jupiter, bringing with it a chance for you to expand your field of social interest. There's a flirtatious feel about this time, too, and, even if you're with a steady partner, you could be rediscovering the charms which attracted you in the first place. On the other hand, if you are single and ready to enjoy yourself, there's no good reason why you shouldn't. Be alert to lucky breaks, one could very well be heading in your direction.

THURSDAY 11th The Moon in Taurus seems to suggest that it is time you paid a little more attention to your cash flow. Certainly, you're very good at spending, but you must admit that when it comes to saving, this is simply a six-letter word you prefer not to think about. If any chance to earn extra cash should come your way, grab it with both hands, because your depleted bank account most certainly needs an injection of cash.

FRIDAY 12th Be on the alert to impulse buying; when you go round the shops in order to buy your evening meal, only to return with some useless article which, at the time, seemed to be a bit of a bargain, is a problem! Remember the old saying, all that glitters is not gold; this is certainly your motto for the day and one you should stick to.

SATURDAY 13th That grey matter of yours is whizzing around like a demented Ferris wheel and, if you are to make any sort of sense out of the day, it will pay you to jot down some notes so that you don't forget them. This evening is a good time for paying visits to those who live close by. No doubt, you will be indulging in a bit of gossip and even scandal-mongering but, as long as you don't go too overboard, there's no reason why you shouldn't enjoy yourself. Brief encounters are a possibility, but don't kid yourself that you've found the love of your life.

SUNDAY 14th   The Full Moon, today, could make life difficult if it's necessary for you to do any short-distance travelling. Often, of course, this is difficult to avoid, but the best thing you can do in order to minimize complications, is to double-check timetables and methods of transport, and leave plenty of time to get to your destination. This evening, some family news may surprise you.

MONDAY 15th   You must stand your ground today and, under no circumstances let other people frown upon your achievements. Neither should you consider the idea of defeat, because the stars suggest that you simply can't lose; all you have to do is believe in yourself, and the world is certainly your oyster. In other words, behave like a typical Aries.

TUESDAY 16th   Your ruling planet, Mars, lines up with mystical, sensitive and subtle Neptune. So you won't be quite so certain about decisions and issues, and this can be no bad thing if it makes you stop and consider the direction in which you're heading. You're highly sensitive, too, and need to spend your time with people who can appreciate you for your real worth, as well as perhaps giving you something of an ego boost. If you're in a special relationship, show how much that person means to you and they will respond with affection, love and a good deal of physical attention too.

WEDNESDAY 17th   The Sun lines up with Mercury and so, if you have been considering signing any sort of document, either on behalf of children or in connection with sports or the arts, you've picked a good time for doing so. You're at your most inquiring at this moment in time and ready to take on new ideas and suggestions, even if they do come from other people. The more active you stay during the day and during the evening, the more stimulating, relaxed and friendly you will become. This can be a good day, it's just basically a case of taking your life in your hands and preparing to take the consequences.

THURSDAY 18th Try to control the crazy impulsive side of your character today. Look back to the past and at some of the mistakes you have made because, if you do so realistically, you'll soon come to realize that it's only your headstrong attitude that has frequently led to unnecessary complications. Once you bring yourself to recognize this, you'll be able to proceed in a more adult and positive way.

FRIDAY 19th As always, and for all of us, life throws up new situations and challenges, and instinctively, today, you should understand that now is the time to begin playing for higher stakes. Deep down you probably don't believe that you have what it takes to compete with others who may be more experienced, but the fact is that rivals are more nervous of you than you are of them. Be ambitious, act tough and the force of your personality should see you through.

SATURDAY 20th Today, there is a danger that you will be far too nice to those who really deserve to be 'ticked off'. What's more, you need some peace and quiet, as well as a space you can call your own; without it, you're unlikely to make very much progress in other areas of life. Your first priority must be to warn colleagues to keep their distance until you've had time to organize yourself. Remember, your own health and peace of mind is more important than the injured feelings of others.

SUNDAY 21st As a fiery Aries, there are times when you let fly with all you've got, and this is one of them. Before you do, though, pause for a moment and work out how much you stand to lose if things don't work out the way you had thought. If it's worth the risk, push ahead and let off steam. If in doubt, you must find a more adaptable and less expensive channel for your anger.

MONDAY 22nd Venus is in a beautiful aspect with Mars and, because of this, you will certainly be seeing life through rose-coloured glasses. Nothing wrong with this in your personal life, but, professionally, you need to fight for concentration because otherwise mistakes can occur. This evening, if you are single, don't waste your time on the television; your charms are apparent, right now, and, if you meet somebody new, this could be the beginning of something really beautiful. If you're in a relationship, it's time to spoil that special someone.

TUESDAY 23rd Although you may feel frustrated at not being able to get one of your ideas off the ground, don't blame others for your bad luck. The fact is that everybody seems to be in the same boat at the moment and arguing about it will only make things worse. Go with the flow today and indulge every passion and whim. Chances to relax and watch the world go by come all too rarely and the chances are that you won't get time to catch your breath in the very near future.

WEDNESDAY 24th Don't expect life to change at present, but do begin looking forward to a brighter and better future. Although the curtain can't be run down on one particular emotional drama, there are no end of things you can do to ease the pressure. Make sure partners and loved ones understand that your need to be alone is in no way a reflection on how you feel about them.

THURSDAY 25th Although you would dearly love to tell others how you really feel, for some reason the words won't come out the way you intended. Best then to keep your thoughts to yourself, but keep practising what you would most like to say, so you'll be word perfect when the planetary picture is slightly better.

FRIDAY 26th   Your ruling planet, Mars, lines up with Pluto today, a rather explosive combination. Yes, it won't take much for you to see red and then, of course, anything can happen. Do try hard to keep control of yourself, particularly when in the company the more gentle members of your circle otherwise, at a later date, apologies will become necessary and that fierce pride of yours doesn't make this an easy thing to do – does it?

SATURDAY 27th   If a friend or a colleague asks you for advice, under no circumstances brush them to one side, even if you're up to your eyes in work. Something they say or do will help you to look at your own problems from a new perspective, and you may even realize that you are not so hard-done-by after all. Always remember there is somebody worse off than yourself, it is only arrogance and ignorance that makes us believe that our problems are in a class of their own.

SUNDAY 28th   With your confidence, there are times when you think you can get away with murder, but if this is the case today, then think again. The stars suggest that partners are not as weak or as willing to please as they seem. Just because you're upfront about what you think and feel doesn't mean others are, too. In fact, if you take too much for granted, right now, you could find you have been out-classed in some way.

MONDAY 29th   This is the day of the New Moon and it occurs at the zenith of your chart which certainly bodes well for pushing ahead with all those ambitions of yours. If you're out of work, you couldn't have a better time for going to interviews and meetings; alternatively it's a time to put some of your ambitious plans into action. You may also become romantically involved with somebody you meet during your working life.

TUESDAY 30th   Today, what you must avoid is turning a bad situation into an intolerable one by tearing through life and preferring to ignore it. There are bound to be situations, when things are said in the heat of the moment, that later you regret. However, perhaps it's time to encourage a bit of a storm in order to clear the air.

WEDNESDAY 31st   Although this is a day when certain people may not measure up to your high ideals or share your sense of right and wrong, if you ignore their opinions completely, things will only go from bad to worse. A thought for the day: 'if you think it's going to rain then carry a large umbrella'.

Happy New Year!

Moon Tables

The Moon and Your Moods

Our moods and, indeed, the strength of our intuition are clearly affected by the Moon. After all, you may ask yourself on occasions, why on earth does a well-balanced person such as me suddenly become bad tempered, frigid, emotional or sentimental on certain days? Well, I'm afraid it is all down to the position of the Moon. Why not try an experiment, and attempt to prove it to yourself?

Glance at the Moon table for any given week or month and then put it away. In the meantime, in your diary make notes of your moods and reactions to situations. Once this period has expired, rescue your book, turn to the Moon tables and you will notice a clear pattern of behaviour developing. You don't need an astrologer to work out that for you, during the week, or during the period whilst you were taking notes, the Moon was, for example, in Scorpio when you were feeling depressed, in Cancer, maybe, when you were feeling romantic and in Aries when you developed headaches and were bad tempered, for example.

Your own individual pattern is likely to be repeated monthly. However, do not give in or be surprised if you are unaffected when the Moon passes through certain signs. It may be, for example, that whilst it makes its way through Aries and Libra, you were neither elated nor depressed. What does this mean? Well, such a happening would merely suggest that these two signs are not particularly prominent on your own individual birth chart.

Female readers will probably like to take note of the fact that very often their menstrual cycle, if of normal length, will begin when the Moon is in the same one or two signs, each month. Why not be a devil and experiment? Give it a try. You have nothing to lose, and you may find out an awful lot about yourself.

FULL AND NEW MOONS FOR 1997

January	9th New in ♑	23rd Full in ♌	
February	7th New in ♒	22nd Full in ♍	
March	9th New in ♓	24th Full in ♎	
April	7th New in ♈	22nd Full in ♏	
May	6th New in ♉	22nd Full in ♐	
June	5th New in ♊	20th Full in ♐	
July	4th New in ♋	20th Full in ♑	
August	3rd New in ♌	18th Full in ♒	
September	1st New in ♍	16th Full in ♓	
October	1st New in ♎	16th Full in ♈	31st New in ♏
November	14th Full in ♉	30th New in ♐	
December	14th Full in ♊	29th New in ♑	

KEY

♈ Aries	♌ Leo	♐ Sagittarius
♉ Taurus	♍ Virgo	♑ Capricorn
♊ Gemini	♎ Libra	♒ Aquarius
♋ Cancer	♏ Scorpio	♓ Pisces

THE POSITION OF THE MOON FOR 1997

Jan	Feb	Mar	Apr	May	Jun	Jul	Aug	Sep	Oct	Nov	Dec	
♎	♏	♏|♐	♑	♒	♈	♊	♋	♍	♎	♏	♐	1
♎	♐	♐	♒	♓	♉	♊	♌	♍	♎	♐	♑	2
♎|♏	♐	♐	♒	♓	♉	♊	♌	♍	♏	♐	♑	3
♏	♑	♑	♓	♈	♊	♋	♌	♎	♏	♐	♒	4
♏	♑	♑	♓	♈	♊	♋	♍	♎	♏	♑	♒	5
♐	♒	♒	♈	♉	♋	♌	♍	♏	♐	♑	♓	6
♐	♒	♒	♈	♉	♋	♌	♎	♏	♐	♒	♓	7
♑	♓	♓	♉	♊	♋	♌	♎	♏	♑	♒	♈	8
♑	♓	♓	♉	♊	♌	♍	♎	♐	♑	♓	♈	9
♒	♈	♈	♊	♊	♌	♍	♏	♐	♑|♒	♓	♉	10
♒	♈	♈	♊	♋	♌	♍	♏	♐	♒	♈	♉	11
♓	♉	♉	♊	♋	♍	♎	♐	♑	♒	♈	♉	12
♓	♉	♉	♋	♌	♍	♎|♏	♐	♑	♓	♉	♊	13
♈	♉	♊	♋	♌	♎	♏	♐	♒	♓	♉	♊	14
♈	♊	♊	♌	♌	♎	♏	♑	♒	♈	♊	♋	15
♉	♊	♋	♌	♍	♏	♐	♑	♓	♈	♊	♋	16
♉	♋	♋	♌|♍	♍	♏	♐	♒	♓	♉	♋	♌	17
♊	♋	♋	♍	♍|♎	♏	♑	♒	♈	♉	♋	♌	18
♊	♋|♌	♌	♍	♎	♐	♑	♓	♈	♊	♋	♍	19
♊	♌	♌	♎	♎	♐	♒	♓	♉	♊	♌	♍	20
♋	♌	♍	♎	♏	♑	♒	♈	♉	♋	♌	♍	21
♋	♍	♍	♎	♏	♑	♓	♈	♊	♋	♍	♎	22
♌	♍	♍	♏	♐	♒	♓	♉	♊	♋	♍	♎	23
♌	♍|♎	♎	♏	♐	♒	♈	♉	♋	♌	♍|♎	♏	24
♌	♎	♎	♐	♑	♓	♈	♊	♋	♌	♎	♏	25
♍	♎	♏	♐	♑	♓	♉	♊	♌	♍	♎	♏	26
♍	♏	♏	♑	♒	♈	♉	♋	♌	♍	♏	♐	27
♎	♏	♐	♑	♒	♉	♉	♋	♍	♍|♎	♏	♐	28
♎		♐	♒	♓	♉	♊	♋	♍	♎	♐	♑	29
♎		♑	♒	♓	♉	♊	♌	♍	♎	♐	♑	30
♏		♈		♋		♌		♏		♒		31